Antón Ponce de León Paiva:
The Wisdom of the Ancient ONE
An Inca Initiation

Antón Ponce de León Paiva

The Wisdom
of the
Ancient ONE
An Inca Initiation

Bluestar
Communications

Woodside, California

Translated by Terry Albriton, Mariel and Chris Helmer
First published in Argentina under the title
Y ... el anciano habló
Copyright © by Antón Ponce de León Paiva

This translation:

Copyright © 1995 Bluestar Communications
44 Bear Glenn
Woodside, CA 94062
Tel: 800-6-Bluestar

Edited by Athene Bengtson
Cover Art by Alfons Yogeshwara Bauernfeind

First printing 1995

ISBN: 1-885394-09-8

Library of Congress Cataloging-in-Publication Data
Ponce de León Paiva, Antón, 1930-
    [Y– el anciano habló. English]
    The wisdom of the ancient one/ Antón Ponce de León Paiva.
        p. cm.
    ISBN 1-885394-09-8
    1. Incas--Rites and ceremonies . 2. Initiation rites–Andes
    Region. 3. Incas–Religion.
F3429.3.R58p65   1995
299' .833--dc20   94-40696

Printed in USA

Dedication

To the children and the elders, who are our future.
I say to my children—to all youth:
you have much to learn from your elders.

Also to
Terry Albriton of San Diego, California
and
Mariel and Chris Helmer of Canada
for the love and interest
put into the English translation

Acknowledgment

*I give heartfelt gratitude to Rolando Ugarte Albarracin—
an excellent man, friend, and brother.*

*My gratitude also includes my dear friends and brothers,
Mario Cutimbo Hinojosa, Washington Echarri Sota, and
Erwin Salazar Garces;*

*My thanks goes to those who, with kindness, encouraged
this humble work;*

*My respectable and dear brothers, Jose A. Rosciano
Holder and Vlado Kapetanovic—two well-known writers
of profound mysticism and human sensitivity—honored me
with their friendship. For this I am humbly grateful.*

*I give special thanks to my wife Regia, for her love and
interest. Her considerate tolerance was crucial to the
completion of this small aspiration.*

*I send up thankful prayers for my parents Antonio and
Otilia, who aren't here anymore. Their silence was an
incentive for me. Their love was an example of service.*

Contents

Foreword

It is said that the truth, under the cover of mythology, is one throughout space and time. From the time when man became man, the truth has been perceived and defied. Starting from a cosmogonic conception, it has always ended in a set of philosophical concepts or religious practices identifying an entity creator and principle for everything. This statement is based upon the fact that all people throughout time and space have similarities in their religious ideas without having communicated with one another.

An example is the mollifying of an insatiable god full of rage and revenge—provoked by the evil actions of his children. This idea gave rise to forms of self-inflicted punishment such as fasting and penitence, and material contributions to organized temples, such as tithing and sacrificial offerings. The sacrificial altar is a universally religious tool, as are divine acts of revenge through floods and fire.

Other universal doctrines are the belief in the immortality of the soul, the idea of mankind descending from one original couple, as well as the divine trinity and the messianic doctrine.

The Andean pre-Hispanic cultures—among them the Inca—also held to these universal beliefs. When the Spaniards conquered the Americas, a polemic began that has lasted until today. The question was whether the ancient people's religion was monotheistic and spiritualistic (as is the case in highly developed cultures), or was it a disorderly, pantheistic, and fetishistic belief system of an underdeveloped, savage, and soulless people? The latter prejudice opened the way for cruel abuses practiced by the conquerors.

It is an irony to deem these people as savages, in spite of the fact that they had developed sophisticated systems of socio-politics, architecture, agriculture, irrigation, and hydraulic manipulation. Their textiles and ceramics also expressed an artistic development. We cannot deny that they were also skilled in the medical arts—particularly surgery, which can be observed in their skull trepanations. Their system of astronomy was impressively accurate. Their calendar, marked seasons, projected the solstices, and indicated other important astronomical events. We can still inspect the *Inti Watanas* (Solar Observatories) that remain on the Incan highlands.

In the Andean pre-Hispanic cosmogony, there are three divine entities; the Spaniards probably assumed that this was a pantheistic concept. The three divinities were *Kon*, *Pachakamaq*, and *Wiracocha*. Kon was the lord of fire, thunder, and earthquake; Pachakamaq was the lord of fertility, agriculture, and soothsaying; Wiracocha was the lord of water. Were these separate gods, a single god with different names, or a messianic succession, still waiting for *INKARRI*, who would rebuild the Inca Empire? This is the unanswered question.

The controversy becomes complicated with the introduction of a fourth Incan cult. Precisely when the Andean civilization was at its peak, the Sun God *Inti* appeared in Incan religion. Inti enjoyed the grandest and most important temple—*Koricancha*, golden enclosure. His *Intiq Raymi*—the Sun Festival at the winter solstice—was the most lavish of the religious events, indicating the importance of this entity.

In the Andean mythology, the Sun was anthropomorphized in a way similar to the Greek god Hyperion. This may suggest to some that the Incas might have been backward in their religious philosophy.

Yet even present day religions share this apparent misunderstanding. As a matter of fact, religion tends to create this confusion because it focuses only on what man can do to placate his god, and fulfill rituals that will assure an easy life. Sometimes these symbols and rituals become part of folklore.

However, there have always been men, who have searched for the Great Truth and the Great Cause; they sought for deeper answers about things and about their infinite destination. Through this search, they have managed to capture part of that truth—to discover the incredible capacity of man that goes beyond the five senses. This capacity, used correctly, enables one to understand the macrocosm and microcosm.

As a consequence of this search, schools, societies, lodges and orders—once thought of as secret and initiate—have come to light. In ancient Peru, of course, there were groups such as the *Orejones,* whose initiating ceremony was the *Warachicuy* (comparable to knighthood in Europe).

El Paititi (the lost city of the Incas) has been a mysterious legend until now. It was here that the Incas were to have hidden all their icons and sacred artifacts—including a golden disc representing the Inti—to protect them from the Spaniards. It is said that the Spaniards only found an insignificant replica of the Inti. El Paititi is still being searched for, but legend says that the city is protected from ambitious people. The Great Andean Chief, Tupac Amaru, the great revolutionary fighter against European pressure, wore the medallion of the Paititi Secret Society. Perhaps he was initiated there.

At present, there are still several indigenous societies such as the Ukukos, Alto Misayoq, Pampa Misayoq, Kallawayos, Intiq Churincuna (Solar Brotherhood), the Seven Rays Brotherhood, etc.

Antón Ponce de León Paiva, author of this book, came in touch with one of these societies and has been initiated, since he was allowed to talk to the "Old Man." He talks to us about a Black Sun that shines only for itself. Something like the philosophy of the visible darkness. Would that sun be the Inti of the Incas and not the sun that gives us light and warmth? The Quechua people have a name for this star: *Apu Punchay* (Lord of the Day Light).

We had better travel with the author, and go deeper inside the message that Nina Soncco, the Anchient One, shares with us.

Mario Cutimbo Hinojosa

Mr. Mario Cutimbo Hinojosa is the principal of the Cusco Ciencias High School in Peru, founded by The Liberator—Simon Bolivar in 1825.

Past History

More than forty years have passed since that day on which I saw for the first and last time Yupanqui Puma who, according to my father, was the descendant of Tupac Inca Yupanqui, tenth Inca of the Second Dynasty, son of Pachacutec. Nevertheless, it seems only a few hours ago that I saw him stretched out on his deathbed. His presence was full of light, and in spite of his aged body, was exceedingly impressive.

At the time, I was seven years old. My days were spent in the security of my family and my little elementary school—where my father was a teacher—number 711 in Urubamba, nestled in the Sacred Valley of the Incas.

My childhood home, located two and a half miles north of town, encompassed about two hectares of land, which were planted with vegetable gardens, grains, fruit trees, and grazing fields for the two cows that supplied our morning milk. We also had sheep, pigs, hens and rabbits. Essentially, it was a small farm. My mother cultivated an enormous variety of roses and other flowers in the well tended garden at the front of the house, where our bees delighted themselves in giving us exquisite honey.

When I turned seven, my father allowed me, as a birthday gift, to graft seven new pear trees; they later provided us with delectable pears. This beautiful spot is the site of what I have come to call *Samana Wasi*, or the

13

House Of Rest and the Abode Of Peace, and by extension, the Place Of Balance and Of Harmony.

The Sacred Valley of the Incas, which actually extends from Huambutio in the south to Machu Picchu in the north, is bathed by the waters of the Vilcanota. Our ancestors called it *Wilcamayo*: (Wilca—sacred; mayo—river). This valley is characterized as much by its pleasant climate as by its multicolored landscape. It charms those who have the good fortune to frequent it, and those who travel there in search of peace or knowledge. Its generous yield provides us with apples, pears, plums, peaches, capuli (similar to the cherry), the delicious strawberry from which a fermented drink named frutillada is made, and corn in all its different varieties—especially a white corn that has a quality unequaled anywhere in the world. This magnificent and varied geographic setting is a pivotal point of the world—a place of light on our planet along the serpentine spine of the Andes. It is here that my story takes place.

Everyday, native peasants came from the mountains to Samana Wasi at approximately five o'clock in the afternoon, to receive lessons from my father. Our living-dining room served as the classroom; the students would sit on the cement floor and I would nestle among them on their ponchos. My father would light four candles,[1] and thus, he began what he did daily: to teach with the patience and love so typical of him. With great understanding and tolerance he corrected the mistakes of those peasant farmers.

"As much as you wish to learn, you will learn," he told them. "Everything depends on you, and all lies within you."

This unselfish, daily work required the sacrifice of any leisure time that my father or the farmers had. They all

14

had families, and not much free time between responsibilities. Determined to improve themselves, these men would arrive, still sweaty from a strenuous days work, to have their classes. The memory of this scenario is as vivid for me as a winter day in Cusco—that sacred, mysterious and grand city the like of which are few in the world. During this daily routine, when the farmers had arrived, they would embrace my father in an affectionate and respectful way. (This might not signify anything special today, but in those times of profound social discrimination and abuse against the Indians, it was extraordinary.) He, in turn, greeted them likewise, as friends who had returned after a long absence. They addressed him directly by his first name and not—according to the custom of the time—as "Sir." After the day's lessons were concluded, they departed with the same ritual of a fond embrace.

My seventh spring had just begun, and with it came the promise of life. At midnight came a memorable but sad event, which I will never forget. My family awoke to a loud knocking at the door and the barking of our two dogs. My father left his bedroom to find out what was happening; I, half-asleep, was right behind him. He opened the door to find a young, slender, and very excited native farmer, who was a stranger to me. He also looked very tired. To protect himself from the cold he wore a red poncho and a woolen cap.

"Mr. Antonio?" he asked after greeting my father.

"That's me," answered my father.

"Yupanqui Puma is dying, and asks that you go to him immediately because he needs to talk with you."

My father was speechless for an instant.

"Wait a minute," he said and went to the bedroom

where he shared the sad news with my mother. She cried as if it were her own father.

"Oh, what a loss!" she lamented as she got up to prepare for my father's departure.

"I want to go, too," I said.

"No," was my father's response. He was usually very indulgent with me, but not this time.

Nonetheless, I persisted so much that he finally gave in and had a horse saddled for me.

At dawn, we headed in the direction of the Pumahuanca Mountains. We passed by the beautiful, triangular Chupani Mesa—also called *Pumacchupan*.[2] It is a small formation, watered by two streams—*Pacchac*[3] and *Sutoc*[4]—that unite at its center. In the darkness, I thought I saw a giant that would trample us at any moment, but it was actually the mountain called *Korihuayrachina*.[5] Korihuayrachina forms the base of a strange, energy-charged triangular plateau; my father often visited the archaeological remains that are there.[6] We continued our journey to *Kunkani*[7] and beyond.

Francisco Uñapilco was the name of the young farmer who guided us. I do not remember my father conversing with him; it seemed to me that they traveled in silence. Every so often, Father would turn his head to look at me while continuing to lead my slow-moving horse by the reins.

We crossed over several mountains. I saw a beautiful lake, small valleys and several rivers (actually streams that looked like rivers to me). After spending the night in a cave, we resumed our journey the next day.

Just as the sun was setting, we came around a mountain and caught sight of a small village situated on another lovely plateau. The path downhill was narrow and dangerous. There were some resting places—look-out points of carved rock that appeared to be of Incan origin—where we would stop for a few minutes. As we approached, we heard more and more clearly some strange and sad songs that gave me goose bumps. In spite of the gloomy atmosphere, the air was perfumed with tantalizing draughts of roses and broom flowers from some unseen garden nearby. Perhaps the rapidly approaching darkness obscured them from sight. I commented on this to my father who confirmed my observations without further comment. The fragrant air caressed us warmly with a light breeze.

It was already dark when we entered the plaza of a small town, and approached a little hut. Some farmers who were leaving the dwelling saw my father, and they approached and embraced him in the familiar fashion. Father lifted me down from the horse and quickly entered the hut; I followed him.

Lying on a bed (more like a platform of sticks and leather) was an old man with long, dark hair and a furrowed, copper colored complexion. Four old men surrounded the bed. Women sang as they sat in a circle in front of the cot on the earthen floor, while men sat on wooden benches against the walls. Guinea pigs wandered in and around the feet of the men. To the left of the door was a fireplace with two large clay pots in which two young women were heating a delicious tea that they invited us to drink. Beyond the fireplace was a ladder made of sticks—the rungs were well worn—that led to the attic where food was stored. A two or three year old boy dressed in a *culi*[8] was near the young women. He was looking distractedly at the people and was certainly unaware of the town's grief over the elderly man's imminent death.

My father was standing in silence looking at Yupanqui Puma, when the old man opened his small, bright eyes and motioned to him with his right hand to come closer. Taking his hand and holding it with love, my father leaned over him to better hear what Yupanqui Puma was saying. Father hugged Puma tightly, and shook with crying as he listened to words that I, of course, could not hear.

For a moment, my father put his head on the old man's chest, then he kissed him on the forehead and stood up. Yupanqui Puma had left his body! He was no longer among us.

The haunting melodies stopped; there was silence. I noticed a large, white, woolly dog lying under the bed. He seemed to be sleeping, nevertheless he was emitting a weak howl, like a moan of pain. Did he have knowledge of the death of his master and friend? My father took a deep breath, and we left the hut, everyone silently crying.

The night outside was beautiful with a clear sky resplendent with stars—one of them moved! The star descended a bit then stopped, and then moved again! I asked what it was.

"It is Yupanqui Puma, who is gone and is now free. He has departed on his last trip with the joy of 'he who leaves to live,'" said my father.

I didn't pursue it, as he was too sad to explain further. Now, I know what he meant.

Our backs were to the hut; I wanted to turn in order to go back inside, but my father stopped me by grabbing my left arm—perhaps, so that I would not witness the ceremony taking place there. Nevertheless, I turned my head and was astonished. The hut was completely illumined as if it were covered by a golden light, that seemed to change to violet and then back to gold again.

I was frightened. I told my father to turn around and look, which he did, but it all seemed perfectly natural to him. He explained, "This is what happens when a man like Yupanqui Puma departs in pursuit of his new mission, completely conscious of reality. Someday you will understand what I am telling you, son."

Once again, I looked up at the sky. The moon was beginning to rise, illuminating the plateau as if it wished to govern the night. One could not feel even the slightest breeze; everything was still—a profound silence. There was peace in the air mixed with a strange joy.

The star that had moved was no longer there. However, in the village square, Indians—apparently praying and meditating—would look at the sky without comment. I found this to be rather unusual. Was this phenomenon, which seemed so familiar to them, such an ordinary occurrence? Did they often see stars that moved? Undoubtedly, we are not alone in the universe; besides, a very important personage had died.

We spent the night in the neighboring hut. I could not sleep; I kept thinking that, at any moment, I might again hear those haunting tunes. I opened my eyes and discovered my room to be so light that I thought it was already dawn. My father was standing and talking with a man who looked like Yupanqui Puma, but…their feet were not touching the ground! It gave me a start!

"What is going on, Papa?" I asked.

"Nothing, son, nothing. Go back to sleep." He hugged me reassuringly.

When Francisco Uñapilco awoke us, it was dawn. The stars were still visible and seemed brighter than last night as we stepped outside. It was a little chilly.

To my surprise, someone was already mounted on my horse, which Francisco had saddled. It was the toddler that I had seen the previous night who had sat next to the fire in the hut where Yupanqui Puma had died.

My father immediately said, "This is Lucas. He is going with us, and you will take care of him during the trip so that he does not fall off."

Father set me behind Lucas on the saddle, and covered us with his poncho as we set out on our return trip. Regrettably, we did not attend Yupanqui Puma's burial, which must have been something quite special. We left the village discreetly. My father held the horse's reins in his left hand and, like someone who does not wish to leave, walked slowly at Francisco Uñapilco's side. Again, they did not talk during the entire journey, or perhaps, I did not hear them.

By sunset, the following day, we arrived at Samana Wasi. Uñapilco did not even go inside, but said his good-byes at the door. He kissed the boy who had ridden with me, and with misty eyes, grabbed me by the head in an affectionate gesture. He and my father embraced each other. I did not see him again.

When we went inside, we found my mother waiting for us anxiously. She listened attentively while my father recounted everything that had happened. It was thus that I discovered just who Yupanqui Puma really was—that incredible personage who, without ever having said a word to me, was to influence my life from that time forward.

Was it Yupanqui Puma who directed my life properly? That is, was it he who showed me the path that I must take and follow during this insignificant interval that we call life on earth and which we naïvely believe to be the only existence?

Yupanqui Puma's age was unknown, but was rumored to be 130 or 140 years old. He had seen the birth and death of several generations. He was a descendent of Inca royalty, and was heir to the Quechua tradition. He was a wise man, a teacher, an initiate, an *Illac Uma*;[9] he was the highest spiritual leader on a progression of seven levels, of the Quechua religion, which still survives hidden in the *chincanas,*[10] invisible to the neophytes and the profanely curious. I had actually met him! What a great and unearned honor!

The four old men who had stood around his bed were his sons. Lucas, who could not be more than three years old, was the youngest of his sons. How unusual this was, and outside of the socially normal standard! Lucas' very young mother had died at his birth, and as his other brothers were elderly men in their eighties or nineties, Yupanqui Puma had entrusted my father with his care, protection and education. From that time on, Lucas grew up as the youngest of my brothers.

Since I was falling asleep, my mother put me to bed while my parents continued their conversation. Having experienced such a lot during the previous days, I fell fast asleep. In my dreams I walked once again on the path we had traveled on Korihuayrachina Mountain, where I met Yupanqui Puma. (I have no idea how I got to the top of that mountain). I ran and embraced him. He hugged me affectionately and spoke to me of many things which I knew. At another point in the dream, I could not see him but I heard his voice.

"Do not try to come back in search of this path because you will not be able to find it." And, so it was.

I asked myself repeatedly what relationship existed between my father and that very special being named Yupanqui Puma—the Illac Uma of a race of genuine builders of a new, more just and equitable society. What was Father's connection with those peasant farmers, who greeted one another in such a special way each time they met my father? Did they belong to some fraternal group or lodge? What bound them together so closely and hermetically that I hadn't begun to realize what was going on until today?

My young head began to fill up with a sea of questions. Who were my real parents? Who was I? Did I really belong to my parents, or was I some being who had sought to materialize in my home to fulfill his mission (as we all do) in this life?

If God did exist, where was He? Why didn't He listen to me? A feeling of profound spirituality—still incomprehensible to me—passionately seethed in me, and moved me to search my unfathomable depths for an answer. I was afraid of death. It terrified me to think that death could claim me at any moment without my ever having understood the life I was experiencing now. I began to look for explanations to those many metaphysical problems.

So many experiences within such a short time had overwhelmed me tremendously. I looked for the answers in the exterior world without realizing that, in that direction, I was beginning to make my first mistake.

Over some thirty years, on more than one occasion, I tried to dispel my doubts by looking for the path that would lead me to that little village where I had met Yupanqui Puma, but I could never find it. On his part, my father maintained total secrecy. Each time I asked him, he evaded my questions by giving the same answer.

"We were friends, and because of that, he left his youngest son in my care. That is all there is to it."

Father kept his secret until his death—a behavior characterized only in those great men who know how to honor their commitments. When he died, all of us children mourned the immense loss of his physical presence, but now we realize that he is fine.

Throughout those thirty years, I enrolled in several schools of spirituality in an effort to find answers to my unknowns, clarity for my doubts which became progressively more numerous and significant. It was in this way that I became familiar with the Rosicrucians, the Gnostics, the Masons, the Anthroposophists, the Theosophists, and other esoteric religions. All of them helped me according to their own strengths. I returned to Urubamba after having been abroad, to look for the path to Yupanqui Puma's village, but I never found it again.

One day, also marked as an important milestone in my life, I found myself once again in Urubamba. I was enjoying a brief vacation with my parents, brothers, and sisters in my elder sister's home. A young peasant—about twenty-five years old—knocked at the door asking for my father. Father went out to meet him.

The young man asked, "Are you Antonio?"

My father smiled, his eyes shining with joy, and they embraced one another just as I remembered from my experience at seven years old. Remembering that experience and observing this scene both at once, I felt as if my heart would leap from my chest. All of the experiences from my childhood resurfaced; it seemed as if I were facing that very Uñapilco. Noticeably moved himself, my father, pointed at me.

"This is my son," Father said.

"Yes, I supposed as much. Everything is as I was told," he answered, looking at me. What moments those were! With great solemnity, my father continued, addressing himself to me.

"Son, the moment you have long awaited has finally come. Accompanied by José Pumaccahua, you will leave for those heights to which you had wanted to return so many times. I lament not being able to go myself—it's my age."

I did not know what to say. I was too shaken and had a lump in my throat. I hugged him tightly. I think we both cried. I had waited thirty long years!

"When do we leave?" I asked Pumaccahua.

"Immediately. We must not waste any time," he answered.

I had just a few minutes to prepare for my trip. I grabbed my canteen, a compass, and an altimeter (which turned out to be useless), a poncho, some notebooks, and other necessities. I said good-bye to my parents, and then headed out, at the stroke of noon, toward the heights of Pumahuanca.

The hills seemed more beautiful than I remembered. There was the path—the path that I had not been able to find for those many years. My eyes had simply looked without seeing the way. I understood then, that the opportunity for me had just arrived.

I wanted to engage José in conversation, but he was so nonverbal that his answers—when he gave me any—were monosyllables, "yes" or "no." I opted to keep quiet. We traveled almost in complete silence. When he did not want me to see or recognize a certain place, he unceremoniously covered my eyes with a piece of black cloth, placed the poncho over my head, and then led me by holding tightly to my arm. I understood it, and with humility accepted his orders; I remembered similar moments that I had experienced.

Our journey of almost three days consisted of climbing up and down mountains, crossing rivers, sleeping in caves, and walking on goat paths. Late at night, we finally arrived at that cherished and long-sought plateau that I had visited in my childhood. Our clothes were completely soaked from a torrential downpour that had caught us two or three hours before. We entered the plaza of the village and then, the little hut that had been reserved for me.

Inside, we found a young woman, twenty-four or twenty-five years old, poking the fire. I greeted her and she answered, looking at me with no surprise. It seemed that they had been expecting me. She had large, black, sparkling eyes that looked like two stars, and without thinking, I made a remark to her.

"Chaska ñahui,[11] *eh?"*

She smiled and left accompanied by Pumaccahua. I had no opportunity to ask whether I would meet Yupanqui Puma's successor that same night. I changed my wet clothing and went over to the fire to get warm.

The young woman returned with food for my meal. I asked her name.

"Call me what you did when you arrived. I like it," she replied and left again. From then on, I always called her Chaska ñahui; I never did learn her real name.

On her way out, she passed Pumaccahua. He had come back to tell me that the chief of the village would receive me the following day; then he left, too. I had no interest in talking with the chief of the village. I wanted to speak with the heir and successor to Yupanqui Puma. As I was reflecting upon this, Pumaccahua returned, bringing me a hot, aromatic, and tasty drink. He spoke as if he had read my thoughts.

"Nina Soncco[12] is our spiritual leader and he is, therefore, the chief with whom you will talk tomorrow."

I thanked him for his troubles. We had been companions on this long, rugged trip, and he still continued to worry about me.

The hut seemed familiar to me. I had the feeling that I had been there before. I fell deeply asleep; I was very tired.

The First Day
Andean Cosmogony: Inti

It was dawn when I awoke. I got up from my bed on the earthen floor, and looked out the door from where I could see the little plaza. How exciting! Nothing had changed; as a matter of fact, my hut was the same one I had stayed in when, as a child, I had accompanied my father. Beside it was the hut where I had met Yupanqui Puma.

I washed in a little stream that I discovered behind the hut. When I returned, Chaska ñahui was already there with a jug of hot milk and some toasted corn bread that she had brought me for breakfast. I thanked her and asked if she might bring me some tea or coffee because I do not drink milk. She was surprised and went out laughing only to return with a delectable infusion of hot tea.

After a brief time passed, Pumaccahua arrived with his customary few words. He beckoned me to follow him and we entered Yupanqui Puma's hut. I felt emotion and great respect for the hospitable atmosphere that I sensed there. Everything was as it had been thirty years ago—the fireplace, the ladder leading to the attic with its rungs even more worn down. I was living the past in a present moment. The past is a creation of the present just as the future is the present of tomorrow.

When I emerged from my reverie, José was no longer there, so I continued to remember incidents experienced in that hut. I turned around toward the door and found myself face to face with an elderly Indian couple who had come in without my hearing them. I was going to greet them when the old man cut me off sharply in Quechua. He was so emphatic that I had no trouble sensing his anger. I was shocked!

"Who do you think you are to judge your father? You always thought that he was not concerned about your questions and anxieties. You do not know the number of times that he asked us to receive you, but he, faithful and true to his word, never told you about the relationship that we maintained—a relationship that unquestionably was and is very important to us."

I felt really ashamed for what I believe had been a self-centered attitude on my part. In fact, on more than one occasion, I had thought that my father had no interest in my aspirations to investigate the sources of the religious beliefs of our ancestors. Every time I had asked a question, he avoided answering. How wrongly had I interpreted his silence!

"How did you dare to think so critically of him who gave you physical life and always looked after your well being with so much tolerance? Don't you think you were unfair?"

In short, the old one said many things to me that I felt dwarfed by his side (in spite of the fact that he was a small man). He became quiet for a moment, then turned toward the bed, picked up a poncho and placed it on a wooden bench. He then put his hand on my shoulder and motioned me to sit down, which I did. He seated himself at my side. The elderly woman, his wife, took both my hands and gave me a beautiful smile as she looked at me affectionately, and then left the hut. It was not until then that I was able to convey my father's greetings.

"Things do not always happen when one wishes," the chief continued in a much friendlier tone, "but rather, when circumstances and conditions are suitable—that is, at the opportune moment—neither before nor after. Arrogance plays with us, making us believe that we have a right to demand."

"Let this be your first lesson: to not prejudge, and learn to wait with humility."

In other words, I think he wanted to tell me "not to fire before taking aim,"[13] I had remained with my head bowed, but as there was silence, I raised it to meet his eyes which were looking at me tenderly, and at the same time, very penetratingly. They were such small, bright eyes like those of Yupanqui Puma. He stood up and extended his arms. I got up, and he embraced me warmly. I reciprocated, very moved, and with profound respect gave him a kiss on the cheek. He stood erect and looked strong in spite of his age. How old was he? I do not know, but I imagine he was past ninety.

"Our meeting was uncomfortable for both of us, but now that is over," he said. "You are here with my permission and approval. I am the successor to our eldest and beloved brother, Yupanqui Puma, whom you met when you were a child, and under circumstances which were very sad for us. Since your birth, we have followed your progress, at your father's behest; we know more about you than you know about yourself. In faraway places, some of the experiences that you have had were foretold."

In that moment, I recalled another teacher whom I had met in Argentina and who had actually predicted several future events that happened exactly as foreseen. I now remember other predictions he made have not as yet taken place.

But, who was this old man, Nina Soncco, whose name so befitted him? Without a doubt, he projected warmth in his words and through his calm and gentle look. I knew that he was another Illac Uma, and to converse with him was a great honor for me, but who was he, really? A wise man who would teach me Andean cosmogony, perhaps? A way of life? Who knows?

"This is the first of seven days during which you will live with us," he continued, drawing me out of my thoughts, "and we shall speak first of Inti[14] in order to better understand everything else we will touch upon during these days."

Thus, began a week of knowledge and reflections, a week in which I discovered who the real Inti, god of our forefathers, was. I had read several national and foreign historians, who were certainly well-intentioned and widely recognized investigators, but very little had been written on Andean religion. Many avoid the subject probably because the most important myths are still hidden; and, therefore, historians are reluctant to discuss a topic that is unknown to them.

Franklin Peace was a dedicated researcher of our history. He referred to the Andean cosmic vision in his book, *The Andean God Creator*:

"The Cuscan chronicles foster the appreciation of a direct link between the creation effected by Wiracocha in his primordial time and the myth of solar origin of the Tahuantinsuyo with Manco Ccapac and Mama Ocllo, founders of Cusco. The Cuscan chronicles tell us of a fundamental creation by Wiracocha who first created Heaven, the Earth and a generation of man who lived in darkness. This initial presence of the god is related to Lake Titicaca from which he emerged. Then the creator disappears (into heaven?) and the men, who as yet have no knowledge of light, sin against him. This first fall brings a new appearance by Wiracocha, the creator, who returns from the sacred lake and destroys the original humanity, converting it into the stone statues in human form that were found at Tiahuanacu. These statues are the "models" for the new humanity that Wiracocha brought forth from the subsoil (rivers, springs, hills, trees, etc.) into the four directions of space."

Besides mankind, Wiracocha created light, sending the sun and the Moon into the Heavens. At the same time, he created the other heavenly bodies as well as the mythological beings.

Other researchers of Peruvian history—among them, Drs. Luis E. Valcarcel, José Sebastian Barranca, Max Uhle, and Julio C. Tello—assert that the Peruvians of antiquity had various deities: Kon, Pachacamac, Wiracocha, and Inti being among the principal gods.

Father Acosta, on the other hand, like the North American author William Prescott, is of the belief that there was only one spiritual god, *Pachacamac*,[15] whom they also called *Pacha Yachachic*[16] or *Usapa*,[17] creator of the universe, incorporeal, soul of the world. Inca Garcilaso de la Vega, a Cuscan of that era, assures us that his noble forefathers were monotheists.

The studies mentioned above, Dr. Valcarcel's, for example, say of the latter three deities, that belief in them suffered from the influence of the Catholic religion imposed by the Spanish conquerors, and because of this influence, the hypothesis of a single god came into being. Other authors affirm that Wiracocha and Pachacamac are, in the final analysis, the sun, i.e., Inti.

Nina Soncco told me, "Our ancestors had many minor gods, but the great deity was Wiracocha who created Inti, the sun God, as his Physical manifestation, life-giver, generator, and creator. As our forefathers felt Inti's physical presence and his benevolent heat that gave light and life, they forgot their true father and began to claim Inti as their principal deity." With this clarification, he continued, "He lives in each one of us; we are Him, that is why we are also creators. The Inti who lives within each human body is complete. At the same time, it is part of the universal Inti."

I wish that he had clarified here what the "universal Inti" was. Did he mean a cosmic Inti? Or, was he referring to the true father Wiracocha? Would I be able to call this a synonym for God?

Soncco continued, "Inti manifests himself when a person is aware of the following:

      1. What or who one is
      2. What life is
      3. What one expects from life

"This triad of unknowns is the first clue to be deciphered by the person who wishes to excel at any activity in this life, or who is in search of spiritual advancement. By doing so, we can understand the path we are to follow in order to accomplish our objectives. We are a divine spark in essence. This spark finds itself locked in the cage of our physical body. Therefore, this body is the temple of a God—the only temple that one cannot change and therefore must care for and respect. The divine spark must exteriorize and manifest itself by illuminating the entire body from the center of the thorax, where it is located, to the last cell that will become aware of its reality, or, its mission. Thus, the body will function in harmony and in balance with the spark."

"Behind the sun that shines on us is then another sun; it is dark, but shines with its own light, and we cannot see it. The one we do see is only its physical manifestation. The other sun is Wiracocha, the God of Gods, the True Sun!"

"This creator, the god Inti, once revealed himself to mankind in human form. He was slender, with long, wavy hair as white as his robe, which was so bright that no one could open their eyes. His beard was also as white as his skin. He manifested himself in this way, but it was not his true form."

After a brief silence, Nina Soncco sighed deeply. He looked at me and smiled. I was completely engrossed, voyaging through unknown worlds of the past. Several hours had gone by, which, nevertheless, seemed short. The topic was so significant, and he had made it so interesting, that I did not realize how much time had actually passed.

Seated on rocks at the doorway of his hut, we ate lunch together and admired the large ceiba tree in the plaza where the red-yellow flowers strewn on the ground resembled a beautiful carpet on which children rested, protecting themselves from the hot sun under the shade of that ancient tree.

Attentive Chaska ñahui took care of our needs. I think she also tended to the general care of the elderly couple. She was an attractive, slender girl; her skin was the color of copper, her eyes were large, impressive, and black; her long hair was plaited in two beautiful braids.

Again, I began to ponder; who was this Illac Uma named Nina Soncco?

"You want to know who I am?" was the sonorous retort that took me out of my apparently secret thoughts. He could read the ideas as they formed in my mind.

"That's right," I responded.

"Tomorrow we will talk about that. We will meet for only half days, because I have other responsibilities, except for the last day, when we will meet all day until evening."

I thanked him and headed back to my hut. First, I stopped at the creek that ran behind it in order to refresh myself. The ice-cold water that ran down from the nearby snow-capped mountains was most enjoyable.

I left the writing pad, on which I had taken notes, near my bed. Then, I went out to walk in the fields where the farmers were still working with joy and hilarity. They invited me to have some chicha,[18] which felt good, as the day had become very warm. During those summer months, the temperature climbed high, in spite of the frequent rains.

I drank two big draughts of the delicious chicha, chatting with the workers while they rested. One of them, who was about my age, remarked that his father had gone to Samana Wasi several times and that he knew my father. My father had taught him to read and write.

I took advantage of this juncture to question them about Yupanqui Puma and Nina Soncco. There was a brief silence as they studied me seriously. The man who had spoken to me about his father said they remembered Yupanqui Puma with great affection and respect. Many of them had never met him personally, but they knew that their parents had spent many hours conversing with him.

They said, "He was a saint. He did strange and miraculous things. Our mothers spoke of him somewhat fearfully because on occasion, they had seen him walking through the air or in different places at the same time. He healed many people with his hands. You could not think negative things because he could read your mind. No one lied to him. He helped our village a great deal. People from faraway places would come to see him and wait for days to be received by him. He was good to everyone, but could be harsh when you made mistakes."

"I imagine," I said, interrupting, "that Nina Soncco is the same."

"Of course," replied the farmer, "he is Yupanqui Puma's successor. You must have made some kind of mistake for him to have scolded you. He also knows what you are thinking and he knows what is going on in all of our lives. Nina Soncco lived by Yupanqui Puma's side for the year before his death.

"He is his father." He pointed to one of his companions, who laughed in a satisfied manner. "Soon Nina Soncco will join Yupanqui Puma."

I could not hide my enthusiasm and interest as I made myself more comfortable on the tree trunk where I was seated. As if sensing my question, he asked, "You would like to talk with the next one, too, would you not? But that is not possible. He is bound to speak with no one for a year regardless of the circumstances. Only upon Nina Soncco's death will he meet with all of the village elders and then he will receive us."

"Of course it would have been very interesting to talk to the successor of Nina Soncco but, if that is the rule or custom, one has to respect it", I said and stood up. I had the feeling that they all wanted to go back to work, so I said good-bye and went back to the village. I sat down near the old ceiba to watch the children playing. The afternoon was waning, and I had spent a beautiful day of great importance in my life.

I heard Chaska's voice calling me. She continued to honor my Western traditions by daily preparing my breakfast, lunch and dinner. This time she offered me a delicious meat jerky with potatoes. I was very hungry.

She was getting ready to leave when I asked her to stay and join me for dinner; I have never enjoyed eating alone. She accepted, and we started what seemed to be a trivial conversation but, after mentioning that she had four siblings (three brothers and a younger sister), she remarked that their father was not presently living with them. For a year, he had been occupied with something very important.

"Could it be that he is in the service of Nina Soncco?" I asked.

"Yes," she answered, surprised. "Who told you?"

"Several hours ago I was at a farm where the men were working, and I met one of your brothers. That is how I learned that no one is allowed to talk with him."

"You will not even see him because, when people from outside are here, he goes somewhere else—usually to a hut far out in the country—where he waits until Nina Soncco calls him. Only my mother is with him and I have to look after my brothers and sister, cooking and cleaning for them; I also attend to Nina Soncco and his wife, because, as you have seen, they are elderly."

The conversation with her was very interesting. She left, and I was alone in the company of endless ideas, doubts, and questions which I needed to organize for the next day. The heat from the hearth warmed everything, so I went to bed and made some notes by the light of a candle. While I was writing, I had the feeling that I was not alone. I saw no one, but somebody was watching me. The candle was burning itself out, so I decided to go to sleep.

The Second Day
Noccan Kani: I Am

Undoubtedly the *Apus*[19] were watching over me. They granted me a bright dawn, full of sun, and a blue sky without a cloud in it.

In the distance one could clearly hear the unmistakable warble of the lark, lady and mistress of the heights. She usually stations herself on the most visible branches of the trees so the other birds must be quiet and listen to her.

Thus began a day full of life, warmth, love; and for me, it was particularly special—the second day of a dreamlike experience that would last seven days.

That morning I breakfasted on a most delicious soup with meat and potatoes served in a *pucu*[20] followed by a jug of coffee that Chaska had brought me. She left, gifting me with a smile as on the previous day. I asked her to accompany me every day for dinner. She accepted.

While I waited for Nina Soncco's summons, I reviewed my notes to see if I had duly recorded everything I had heard. When I finished, I looked up and found him standing at the door watching me. Behind him, a very soft violet light could clearly be distinguished. Was it the daylight coming with him into the hut, or what was it? I stood up to greet him and he answered with a peculiar and symbolic gesture of his

38

arms and hands. He turned around and started toward his hut. I followed.

Having invited me to sit down, he spoke.

"You want to know who I am? Well, I will simply tell you, *Noccan Kani*.[21] When you come to understand, assimilate, and become conscious of what these words represent, you will live fully in freedom, and you will be yourself. Because, you also have Noccan Kani within you—unrealized. When that happens, you will know P. K. about whom you will speak to no one. The humanity of today ought to know and to practice the Noccan Kani in order to grow; lamentably, the majority have no interest in saving themselves and will spend their lives on earth without transcending their worldly selves. This is their opportunity; this is your opportunity—learn and teach. You must be yourself as I am, like this (he placed his hand at the center of his chest over the sternum)."

I did not know whether to laugh, or what attitude to assume because I understood nothing. He realized my confusion immediately, and with gentleness and understanding, he continued speaking.

"Generally, the man who knows himself somewhat externally believes that he is his physical body, and he forgets or does not know that within that body is He, Inti."

I wondered whether or not he was referring to the soul.

"I am Inti's son, just as is every creature of creation. For that reason, Inti is within me and I am Inti. Inti is immortal. It is what survives death. The physical body dies and decomposes. I go to *Hanan Pacha*[22] or *Ajay Pacha*;[23] therefore, what is real is Inti, which does not change. That is I am.

"For this reason, I tell you that I am what I am in essence—Inti. And you are the same except you have not

39

known it until now. You must become consciously aware of this principle which is the only truth, then your life will change profoundly. That is, you will be yourself, and your attitudes will be more positive in all physical or psychic relationships and spiritual activities that you engage in. It is, therefore, important that you be what you are in the depth of your being and not what you appear to be. It is now time to be who one is. In this way, you will be consciously free and you will be a part of everything."

"To be truly is to be in everything. Time and space will disappear. Your thinking will take you wherever you wish to go; wherever your thinking is, there you will be. It is important that you take your true place of evolution in order to be happy. When you are, you will know genuine free-will, so be as soon as possible, or the reality of what you were, what you are and what you will be shall continue being unconscious, and you will live as a slave without freedom."

"Father!" I said to myself, "Help me. Manifest in everything I do. I need to enter into silence to be able to listen—to you or to myself, I don't know. But I do know that while I am attentive, you may take form and be revealed. You are in my heart. You are the Christ essence within me; you are the truth in me, and I am You, but—what am I saying?!"

At that moment I realized that Nina Soncco was quiet and was surely listening to my thoughts.

He smiled and said, "It is the truth. You need to be aware of this higher reality, and then you will be protected; whatever you want will be given to you. Your Inti, or whatever you wish to call it, will manifest. You will feel its strength and power. When you receive its messages, you will be able to put them into practice for the good of all your brothers. Be attentive to every insight that comes to you: everything that uplifts, everything that liberates, everything that unites comes from Inti and is good. You need no other advisor.

"Your life is very important. Your mental and physical health are very important. You are very important. Thus, first it is you, then everybody and everything else. What I am telling you is not selfishness, because if you are well, you will radiate that well-being to others, and everyone will benefit. We have come to this earth to be happy and we should be, come what may. With all of our problems, defects and difficulties, we must learn to go through life smiling and believing that our experiences are for our growth. Thus, with our higher understanding, we will suffer less. You will have physical, emotional, mental and spiritual well-being. Whatever you desire will manifest. If you want to live in limitation, such will be your life. If you want to be ill, you will become sick. If you are satisfied with half a piece of bread, you will not have the possibility of obtaining more. If you approach an activity with negativity, the result will be negative. *I am perfection*, and without pride and with great humility I accept this truth which is Inti within me or rather, within this body. All divine power, all divine love, *I am* that life presence. Understand this and then teach your brothers with peace and calmness to discover this, which is the principle of the Light."

"You will see how the depressed, the grieving, the pessimistic, the afflicted may overcome their problems and become realistic. It is the best remedy for their minds, their feelings and their bodies. If you allow your true identity to develop more and more each day, you will see that it becomes discernible to others as a radiant aura around you."

"Noccan Kani is all that exists. It is the center from which you can be just, balanced and harmonious. Place yourself always in the middle path—extremes are harmful and may lead you to fanaticism. Before initiating his activities, a politician ought to think fundamentally about this reality which, once found, has the necessary strength to impose itself on any sectarian doubts or fears, and then to resolve them. Perhaps the politician may teach others to do the same."

"Of course," I interrupted enthusiastically: "God's real name, given by him to all mankind, is 'I Am,' and it appears in the Bible—Exodus, 3:13—'I Am.' 'You are gods,' Jesus said, according to John, 10:34."

"To the extent that you practice reflection, will your false beliefs disappear so that your *real self* will rise into a world without limitations," said Nina Soncco. "Thus, you will also learn not to criticize, judge, or condemn, and you will refrain from hurting anyone with your words or feelings. You will be gentle, tolerant, understanding, respectful and skillful in understanding others. Within your body, which is a temple, is *you*, immortal Inti, flame of eternal life. It is time to identify yourself with what You Are. It is time for you to be free. You cannot settle with being merely like everyone else. You are where your thought is; touch thought with eternal realities; who you are and who you will be will follow."

"You are not the name that you now have although your first and last names are important, and have their own particular sound, vibration, and influence. Each child carries in the electrons a vibratory frequency that has much to do with one's name. The mother feels this vibration, which records itself in her mind, and she gives the child a name that corresponds to its life in this incarnation. Sometimes the father's or the family's pride dictates that the child be given another name and then, he or she may suffer a life of setbacks, frustrations, imbalances and disharmonies. An individual will often not be able to tolerate such a delay and will eventually change one's name, thus restoring the incarnation to the appropriate path on which to fulfill one's destiny."

"The most important name that you had in the last three incarnations was I. A. Uma. You lived near a river sacred to other people."

I wondered if this were perhaps the Ganges in India.

"There you lived until you were seven, with your parents, an older brother, and a younger sister. Then, you went north to the city of Jullundur. As a youth, you left home to go further north to a distant and foreign territory where you met Y. I., with whom you lived a tremendous drama that impacted your consecutive lives until the present—so much so, that the two of you still remember this story. You met again, did you not?"

"That is correct, Master," I answered with surprise. From that moment on, I addressed Soncco in that honorific way.

Indeed, Y. I. and I had met each other in a very casual way in Lima. When I told this middle-aged gentleman about a recurring dream I had, he began to cry, and interrupted me so that he could continue the story that both of us knew and had lived in together, approximately

43

two thousand years before, in Asia. How very emotional had been that moment when we met!

"Now you know who you are," continued Nina Soncco, the master. "Not just a body or a name—which, of course, are important to your physical manifestation— but something greater. It is something of which you should become aware through your feelings, your mind and your bodies."

I had to assume that he meant the physical, etheric, astral, mental, and soulic bodies that I had learned about in the esoteric religions.

"To achieve peace and harmony in all of your affairs, your eyes should see only the good, your ears should hear only the positive, and your lips should speak only the just. Your hands should always work to heal, and your body should always be willing to serve as an in- strument to carry the message, that you now know, to the world. Inti will manifest itself, but not exactly in the way expected by the majority. You have heard it now, so pay attention and tell your brothers in such a way that he who hears you will understand and accept truth and reality. If they do not, what does it matter if you have to repeat it as often as is necessary? Only those who do not want to stand up and start again are in dan- ger.

"Do not miss a single opportunity. Live with enthusi- asm, fully, without depression, and do not permit any- one to be depressed. We have come to be happy, and so we should be. Every day should be a celebration. Enjoy it in spite of your sorrows and difficulties. Life is the highest expression of existence, and we must learn to convert what is bad into something good, and to turn sadness into joy. We must break the chains that bind us to negativity. Everything will be possible if you become aware of your true identity. Right now you probably do not know of what you are capable of and of the immense power that exists inside you. When you discover it, you will live the true reality: Noccan Kani."

Then he began to whisper very softly a melody that turned out to be a mantra that had a startling effect on me. He asked me to try to repeat it with him, which I did several times. It was another teaching that I silently use to assist me even today. Each time that I say the mantra internally, I seem to hear him. Every time I repeat it aloud, I hear his voice accompanying me.

We had lunch together in the same place as on the previous day. Afterwards I left, thanking him, with even greater respect for his teachings. Undoubtedly, I was in the presence of a master. What additional surprises would I have in the days to follow? Would I be able to communicate adequately everything I was hearing? Would people believe me?

I reflected upon these matters as I made my way toward the stream behind the hut. The running water was so crystalline that it allowed me to see, in the bottom of its riverbed, multicolored rocks of various sizes. I sat down on the bank to contemplate how the stream meandered among the huts until it lost itself, and how the children amused themselves jumping from one bank to the other.

I entertained myself all afternoon and even participated in a game with the children—we threw little leaves into the water as if they were boats competing in a race. How much fun the children had following the progress of the race! Of course, I also felt happy seeing their joy and sharing in their euphoria until Chaska appeared to remind me of the time. The children wanted to continue playing but it was already late, so I offered to play the game some more the next day.

Chaska and I had dinner together as agreed. I asked her what her father's name was.

"Like Yupanqui Puma," she answered.

"It is just that I did not know his name," I stated.

"You want me to talk about my father, but I cannot—except to tell you his name: 'Amaru.'"

"What a symbolic name!" I thought. "I hope to have the opportunity to meet him on another occasion," I told her.

She did not answer, but got up and invited me to have that delicious tea served in a mug. Then she left as I thanked her for the meat and her company.

I remained there for several minutes contemplating the fire in the hearth that warmed the entire room. Then, I dedicated myself to organizing my ideas as best I could. I had a vague notion of the important and transcendent themes touched on by Nina Soncco that morning. I needed to reflect a great deal to understand clearly the extraordinary vision of this Quechua master. I was tired and the candle had nearly burned itself out, so I decided to go to sleep.

The Third Day
The Seven Rays

I got up very early, before Father Sun had come up to govern and give life to this new day, which promised to be as beautiful as the previous one, and—of course—equally as productive. On my walk I met several farmers on their way to the fields; some of them were singing, others whistling. They greeted me in a familiar way which pleased me as I supposed that they no longer considered me a stranger.

How delicious is the cherry-like capuli at dawn. Well, it is delicious at any time, for it retains the dew of the night and the chill of the dawn.

I could feel the sun coming up. To its first rays, I lifted my arms as I had been taught and assumed the position of a person in prayer to thank him for having given me this opportunity, and to greet him with the respect and love of son to father. The air was full of life and energy.

"At this hour, the air is always filled with much energy, and one should breathe deeply," I heard the voice of Nina Soncco who had been standing behind me observing. I greeted him.

"In these places, we still breath clean air. The people of the cities should go out to the country often to give their lungs a dose of life."

Was he referring to the ether, or prana, I wondered.

We returned to the hut where we found his wife and Chaska, who was cooking something delicious in the hearth. It was a kind of potato soup, which I liked very much. I told her that she had a talent for guessing my preferences in food.

We ate, and drank piping hot coffee in steamy mugs then Chaska left with Maria, Nina Soncco's wife.

"There are two paths along which we all travel in this life: the first one has definite colors and has existed since man appeared on this planet; the second one is formed by each one of us individually at the moment of birth and we give it the color of our actions."

"*Ccanchis* (seven) is a magic and sacred number manifesting in everything that transcends; it is composed of *Tawa* (four) and *Kimsa* (three) which are also sacred numbers. And so it is that the first path has seven colors. Each person belongs to one color on this path, and that determines one's character and inclinations; therefore, when you learn to see inner realities, you will have an idea what an individual is like.

"Seven farmers, each belonging to a specific color, will be coming here so that you may observe, distinguish and realize the differences that exist among them."

I had to wonder again, was the Master referring to the Rays that I had studied in the other schools? I tried to assimilate this new information with what I had already learned.

Here, I feel the need to explain the concept of the Seven Rays, as I have studied them. There are seven colors, and each person belongs to one, that is, to one type of energy, to a current of power that comes from Inti. Our existence unfolds in one of the seven great Rays of Life

48

that defines us individually. These Rays include specific, determined vibrations and dynamism governed by Inti.

Each ray is also a particular sign of one of the great Initiatic Orders of antiquity (e.g., the Essenes, the Rosicrucians, the Masons, and the Gnostics). These are occult religions that somehow have influenced the progress of the world. The purple ray, for example, led the Essenes out of the desert.

Being a manifestation of Inti, the Rays are an expression of the various aspects of its strength, of spiritual cosmic energy, and of the celestial fire, living symbol of sovereignty. They also correspond with the seven musical notes of a western octave and with the colors of the rainbow.

Undoubtedly, the number seven reveals itself in everything just as the master explained. The important stages in man's development are grouped into seven year periods. The principles of the laws that govern us are seven. The age of the balanced, harmonic person is seven times seven. The energy centers—or main chakras—also number seven; they are the crown, the third eye, the throat, the heart, the solar plexus, the sacral and the root. The glandular organs—pineal, thymus, thyroid, adrenal, pituitary, pancreas, and spleen—receive influences from the chakras and are associated with them. I think it necessary to recall the colors of the seven Rays and their connections to the chakras and to the glands, and the characteristics of each one of them.

The First Ray—crystal-blue—is linked to the crown chakra and the pineal gland. It represents the will of the Father, God, or Inti; therefore, it symbolizes protection and strength. The majority of ambitious executives belong to this ray, as do those who are aggressive and those who desire to dominate.

The Second Ray—golden yellow—is related to the heart chakra and the thymus. It represents wisdom, enlightenment, and love. Mostly teachers belong to it, but so do those who have intellectual pride.

The Third Ray—pink—is connected to the throat chakra and the thyroid gland. It is the Ray of activity, of Divine Love, and, therefore, of beauty. It is very magnetic; it attracts. Peacemakers, arbitrators, but also libertines belong to it.

The Fourth Ray—white—is located in the center of them all, and separates them (the blending of all colors results in the color white). It is linked to the root center and the adrenals. It represents purity, art and harmony—the purification of human beings in ascension. It lightens the darkness. To it belong the majority of the artists, as well as, the bohemians.

The Fifth Ray—green—deals with the third eye and the pituitary gland. It is the Ray of truth and of health. It plays a part in healing and concrete knowledge. In general, medical doctors and inventors belong to this Ray, but so do atheists; as in everything, there are the dual aspects: black-white, positive-negative.

The Sixth Ray—gold-ruby—is related to the solar plexus and the pancreas. Its main characteristic is peace; devotion is another of its qualities. It is said that Jesus belonged to and acted within this Ray. It is, then, the Ray of serenity and patience. Priests and healers belong to it; nevertheless, religious fanatics and snobs may belong to it.

The Seventh Ray—violet—is linked to the sacral center and the spleen. It is the Ray of transmutation, that is, of liberation, of ceremonial magic, and of alchemy. It represents forgiveness par excellence. Violet is the color of this Era. To it belong mostly the mystics, but vanity is also present. It is said that this Ray will allow the Earth to liberate itself and evolve to another plane. Another orbit, perhaps?

Human consciousness will ascend on the individual level, until the true initiation—the real one, the transcending one—is accomplished within each of us. This is a great opportunity for everyone; it is the awakening. The subconscious will open up in revelation, and we shall remember all of our past incarnations. We shall be able to look back and read the akash—or nature's memory—like a book, or view it like a movie. It is then, the gold of our lives.

❦

At that moment during my reverie, seven men with smiling faces entered and drew me out of my reverie. I responded to their greeting with a smile. They sat down on two wooden benches in front of me, waiting to hear Nina Soncco's voice.

He told me, "These seven brothers whom you see, belong to a different color within the same path that I mentioned. Observe them, and in their faces you can see."

I looked at them for a long while without seeing anything in particular. All of them looked the same to me, with small differences of hair, color, age, height, and eyes. They were farmers with the heat and the flavor of the land in their hands, but beyond that, there was nothing that drew my attention. The master was aware of my confusion, of course, and helped me telepathically.

"Of course!" I exclaimed. "There they are! Is that it?"

He nodded his head in affirmation.

"Their manifestation is physical and therefore, it is visible in them. With others, it is more difficult because it is beyond the visible range of our eyes."

I correlated his statement to a description of the double ether.

"Later, I will teach you how you can practice in order to be able to see," he said.

It was a great experience for me, a discovery that would help me later to understand people better. Perceiving my enthusiasm, he asked the seven men to leave, and continued speaking to me about other signs that individualize us even further, differentiate us one from another.

"Do not feel uncomfortable if you do not know something," he told me. "To undertake a task, you will first study, then you will practice; that is, you will have to prepare yourself in order to carry out any particular activity. You are here to learn, and that is what you are doing. The majority of the people are thrown to the task of living without a compass, without preparation, without orientation—blindly, without even having an idea of what life is and, worse than that, without knowing who they are. They do not understand why the differences exist among human beings. They do not understand why some people live in opulence and most live in poverty; why some are physically normal and others are handicapped. They do not look for an eternal justice and equality; they only see the short term appearance of unprovoked suffering. Consequently, they become renegades, creating a disaster of their existence in this Kay Pacha.[24] Whatever you think will be manifested. It is your attitude which determines everything that happens. This is your reality, not the Great Reality."

(My father used to say something similar: "Thoughts acquire form. They are things. What you see is your own concept. If you think you are healthy and strong, you will be so, no matter what you may do. Everything that happens to you is a result of your beliefs and what you say in words. If you have the idea in your mind that you will be robbed or that you are going to have an accident or that you will have good or bad luck, your life will be governed by these conditions and they will manifest themselves in everything you do." This is what my father said daily to the farmers who came down to Samana Wasi.)

"In our heads, there are many ideas of which we are not conscious," Nina Soncco continued. "They are deep within and spring forth from impressions that we receive and in accordance with what we are taught and what we hear, read, and see. Let us be careful, then, about what we accept. Let us not blame Inti for all that happens to us. These things are our creations. We have allowed them to be, so they are. We are born with free will, with the right of choice, and we choose whatever we please: to think well or bad, to be pessimistic or optimistic, positive or negative. All of this is revealed on the outside as well as the inside of our being. In other words, whatever we want, wish or believe most frequently, becomes deeply imbedded in our minds, and awaits our command to manifest itself."

I supposed that he was referring to the subconscience which is a cold and faithful servant; it does not accept jokes—only commands which it obeys.

"What happens is similar to when the mother tells the child not to take off his coat because he may catch a cold. That is the order which goes immediately to the innermost mind of the child. The child takes off his coat and catches a cold because that was the command to his subconscious mind. The mother comes back and re-emphasizes the order by saying, 'You have taken off your clothes, and that is why you have caught a cold.' That is how it works."

How right he was!

"Tomorrow we will continue by talking about other things that are important and that you need to know in order to be more responsible."

We lunched together, which signified to me that he had some regard for my company. Then I left him to other concerns but not without first thanking him again for everything that I was receiving from him, which would certainly be of great value to me in the future.

I heard the voices of children behind the hut and remembered that I had offered to play with them again that day, so I left my notepad and went looking for them. They were already waiting for me. We spent a most enjoyable afternoon, but the children exhausted me. Children are tireless; they possess an energy that is not consumed by any amount of exercise. Happily, Chaska and the evening arrived almost at the same time, and saved me, since the children had wanted to go on playing.

Chaska and I had dinner together as on previous days. The food was very tasty and the conversation very pleasant. She told me that Soncco's wife, Maria, in spite of her age, sang with a very clear and beautiful voice. Her songs related stories from the past about work, love, and the Imperial City. I asked Chaska to sing something that she had heard, which she did. The verses went something like this:

"Gently the wind parts the morning of a quiet
and sleepy sun day while the sun with its
pale rays bathes our Cusco, still asleep."

She sang the words to a lovely, rhythmic and romantic piece of *huaino*[25] music, but did not wish to continue. She nevertheless told me that the lyrics referred to the earthquake suffered by the Sacred City in 1950. We said our good-byes and she left. I organized my ideas a little, and fell asleep. I was very tired.

The Fourth Day
The Seven Principles

I felt very cold as the day dawned raining with that kind of drizzle that seems to have no end but which, at the same time, gives us the chance to breathe very deeply. It seemed as though I had a better capacity to change the seldom replaced residual air of my lungs.

Bundled up in my poncho, I went outside to bathe in the stream, where, to my surprise, I found several children playing at that early hour as if it were not raining. I undressed as I was accustomed to doing at Samana Wasi while the children imitated me, laughing, and went right into the water as if it were not cold at all. I, on the other hand, barely got wet because the water was freezing. I returned to the hut immediately to get warm.

Chaska was already bringing the vegetables and potatoes with jerky to a boil. It smelled delicious. In another pot was water certainly for coffee. She answered my greeting without turning her head. I asked her what was planned for today.

"Nina Soncco must be on his way already," she said. "He is having breakfast here with you, and I did not awaken until just a few minutes ago."

"This is really a surprise!" I exclaimed. "Today we are having a very important guest."

No more than five minutes had passed before the master arrived. He seemed taller and full of light. With him came a very soft aroma of Andean flowers that pleasantly filled the entire hut. I hugged him with great affection and he responded in kind.

"This is your fourth day with us," he said to me, "and you know that *Tawa* (four) is a special and sacred number for us. It represents the most important part of our physical manifestation, symbolizing earth, water, air and fire—the four elements that constitute our body. Thus, during the course of a year, we celebrate various festivities related to earth, water, air and fire. You will witness one of these ceremonies before you leave."

I knew that he was describing some sort of initiatory experience.

Chaska served us the delicious soup of hot vegetables, potatoes and jerky for the cold morning, followed by coffee with corn toast. She tidied up the room a little while we were eating and then went off in the direction of Nina Soncco's hut (probably taking Maria's breakfast to her). She returned later to finish her chores.

"When something bad happens to us," continued Nina Soncco, "only then do we remember the Father, and ask Him to help us. Sometimes He takes care of things and sometimes He does not (or at least, that is how it seems). In the latter case, we are told we must resign ourselves, that it is God's will. In other words, if it is the will of the Father that we suffer, it can be inferred that He is mean, vindictive and rancorous—right?

"It is totally absurd to think in this way. Our ignorance makes us see things from this perspective. It is also the most convenient way for the majority, so that they do not have to analyze and reflect on the real causes of some disagreeable event.

"All religions say that God is good, loving, generous, charitable, etc.; then, how can one believe that He desires our misfortune? We humans would never condemn our children to hell, and with even more reason God, our Father Creator who is the only Perfect and Absolute One in existence, would never do so to us. It appears, then, that we should revise our thinking somewhat. Contradictions exists.

"He gives us daily warmth and life through His physical manifestation, Inti, and nevertheless, we believe, as is convenient for us, that He is good one minute and bad the next. He is neither bad nor good, but plainly and simply, righteous. What happens is that we do not recognize or we forget the provisions that govern and protect everything created by Him; our actions are subject to those principles.

"You may free yourself from human justice depending upon 'who you know' or how much money you have. But from these other laws, there is no way out. If you do good, you will reap great rewards; if you do evil, you will have to suffer the consequences. Hence, it is better to learn, once and for all, to think and to act correctly in accordance with the law in order that all of the good we wish for ourselves and for others can be realized.

"I have already told you that inside our minds, in the deepest part, exists a very serious servant that does not discern or have opinions, that neither thinks nor decides for itself, but only follows orders. It is there that we must send our positive thoughts—all of the good ideas which interest us, or which have the greatest impact upon us—so that they get recorded, and may later manifest themselves consciously when we wish or need their assistance. It is, in other words, a great filing system that never rests nor has any limitations in its receptive capacity.

"How sad! Many relationships fail because the individuals do not know who they are and much less who the other person is."

<hr />

These observations by the master Nina Soncco brought to mind other reflections that belong to the great philosophers and thinkers on earth, our small home. They agree that, if we were to understand our purpose and our meaning in relation to God, or even to Humanity—leaving God out for the moment—we would automatically achieve social harmony and peace. There would be no wars, conflicts, quarrels, or poverty because we would all know that we would not need to be greedy or competitive, violent, or afraid. When you think about your fellow man, you are already relating to God with the Divine Spark that lies within all of us. But it is easier if you begin by understanding who you are because that is where cosmic justice intervenes.

We should not limit ourselves merely to considering this current life as if it were the only one that we have lived. Our previous lives have molded us. We are the product of all of the lives that we have lived. Or, as Pythagoras said: 'Everything is necessary for the development of the soul.' Whoever understands this truth will have probed the depths of the Great Mystery. Make time for yourself to do nothing—to enjoy a sunset, to listen to the song of a bird, to observe the flight of a bee, to listen to your own thoughts, to listen to your neighbor. Otherwise, you might create an empty life—full of things and activities, but empty of progress.

Shakespeare wrote, "To thine own self be true." Have the courage to know yourself, and you will be free. Do not look at my eyes nor my face nor my hands, for that is only the thing wherein I myself live.

Finally, Krishnamurti said, "Each person is a universe. If you know yourself, you know everything. Neither the past nor the future concerns me. I think, act and live for the present which was created from the past and is in the process of creating the future."

How great is the similarity between these truths and the teachings of the master Nina Soncco! The laws or the Principles that he mentioned were basically the same as the ones that I had received and learned through the writings of other teachers whom I had previously had the honor of meeting. The differences were very small and more in their form than in their actual content.

<hr/>

Intuiting that I was already familiar with these concepts, Nina Soncco said, "They are universal and immutable. There is nothing new under the sun, but it is very important to remember and to live in accordance with them."

At that moment I recalled the words of the *Kybalion*:

"The Principles of truth are seven;
He who understands this perfectly
possesses the magic key through which
all gates of the Temple
will be open wide."

Well known in the esoteric world, the *Kybalion* is a marvelous book which gathers all the hermetic philosophies taught in ancient Egypt and Greece, extracted from the tradition left by Hermes Trismegistus and written by Three Initiates. I do not refer to Hermes, god of chance and wealth, he who brought the message from the gods in Greek mythology, but rather, to Hermes Trismegistus, the Three Times Great, Egyptian god, Thoth, fount of wisdom and origin of all culture. It seems that he was a mythical, Egyptian king from the twentieth century before Jesus Christ. Inventor of all the sciences. According to serious scholars of Hermes Trismigestus, only fragments of his writings are preserved, some in Greek and others in Latin. They were discovered on the walls of Temples and on ancient papyrus, which some believe were found by an Egyptian and handed down to his heirs, although others believed that they were found by a Gnostic sect. It is certain, though, that this doctrine influenced alchemy and magic. It is philosophical and astrological. It is a cosmogony and an eschatology that becomes more relevant every day because it helps us to better understand the meaning of life, the universe and God!

Nina Soncco continued, "Everything begins in your head. As you think, so you are. All that you wish for will be if you want it. It starts as an idea that acquires form from the strength and love that you give it until it materializes. That is why I tell you that what you think is very important. Everything—the universe, the earth, man, all that exists—was created in this way by the force of Love. Everything is Inti who is the Creator. We are His image, we are creators.

"In your subconscience is what you believe your life should be. If you nurture it and give it warmth, you will not be able to alter the outcome, good or bad, and it will manifest itself externally so that you will see it. It is deeply lodged in your head working to produce its external equivalent. This belief is not necessarily divinely true, but it is the one that will realize itself because it is the one you believe. You have created your world mentally just as The Father has created everything that exists with his mind. Thoughts acquire form, they are 'things.' They manifest themselves outwardly as health, well-being, rewards, work, optimism, happiness, or as illness, malaise, obstacles, punishment, pessimism, sadness, disgrace—all depending on what one has chosen to think, feel, or believe. That is to say, the only one responsible for what happens to you is you, except for those cases in which other factors intervene that may be social, political, religious, or events which are beyond your control or decision. In general, you cause everything that happens to you, depending upon the mental environment you have created and by which you live. If you are happy, cheerful, contented and optimistic, you will reflect all of that in your attitudes and will radiate congeniality toward others in spite of any obstacles that you may have in your life. You will overcome them with your positive decision.

"As you can see, your mental attitude is very important. You were born with free will, and you freely choose whatever satisfies you, for better or for worse; because, that which you decree will occur, what you accept will realize itself, and what you deny will not happen. Everything depends on your way of thinking, and that way of thinking will be seen externally. If you nourish something properly, you cannot avoid having it grow. If you think in a specific way, you cannot avoid the consequences. It is, therefore, extremely important to learn to differentiate the truth from falsehood, both in your own thinking and in the world.

"It largely depends on the thought that you hold. You will judge according to how you think and according to the crystal you see through. If you exchange the negative viewpoint you have for a more positive concept of things, the transformation will be evident in you face and you will have better comprehension. You will see the people with whom you deal in a more generous light. The change in you will have taken place and your vision will be different. You will view people with greater love and respect. Unquestionably, you must change your mental attitude (that mental attitude which is energy in constant motion, in perpetual activity and unending transformation), and everything will be transformed. Sometimes it is somewhat difficult to accept that everything is mental first and material afterwards—that is—the thought precedes the action.

"Life itself obliges man to study in ever greater depth the causes and beginnings of his origins which are not clearly known even today. The understanding gleaned through his senses is very limited. He requires his mind to discover the vast and the minute. Behind all that exists, is there not a Creative Mind?"

He finished talking and looked at me fixedly. I did not know what to say; I only succeeded in mentioning that my father often repeated the same thing with different words to his students/brothers who came daily to Samana Wasi from the nearby mountains: "If you want to learn, you will learn. Everything depends on you and lies within you."

As if he had not heard me, Nina Soncco resumed his talk. "Let us speak of another teaching. This small world, our body, is similar to the great world, the universe. What happens up there, occurs down here inside us. Also, by studying man, we shall come to know and understand the universe; studying and observing our earth, we shall also comprehend and glimpse other, better worlds."

I thought that perhaps he was referring to other planes of existence.

"The future exists in the present. Within ourselves are also those other worlds, which we do not yet understand, but with which we will become familiar and learn to live in as we progress. Of course, at this moment, we do not have a precise idea of those superior worlds because we are living under other conditions, in a more dense world, and we do not accept their existence. For example, in a drop of water thousands of microscopic creatures live whose existence does not last beyond a few seconds, nevertheless, in that time, their experience is total. Suppose that we were to converse with one of them, and were to tell him that life does not last merely seconds, but rather, fifty, eighty, or more years. He would not believe us, of course, because his reality is another one, even though what we are experiencing is real.

"The same thing happens to us when we are told and assured that there are other beings, similar to us, who live much longer and under different circumstances. We do not believe either. If we talk with an ant whose mind is nothing more than instinctive, we will have to converse with it taking into consideration its level of consciousness. We would inform it, for example, that we work as it does, that we have some similar needs, but no more than this because it would not understand us. Nevertheless, I have to tell you that in spite of those limitations, in each state of life, at every stratum of existence, there are beings that are more advanced than the others in their level, and who are ready to move on to another state. They do glimpse and have a premonition of superior conditions. If we apply this very important principle, many worlds that we do not know will be more comprehensible to us. We shall be able to draw back the veil that hides the unknown from our vision so that we may relate to our cosmos.

"There is something perfect in us that is just waiting for the opportunity to reveal itself: Inti, who is immortal, as you know. On the other hand, our physical body begins to die as soon as it is born. Within each child there is an elder and there is death, but within both lies eternal life. The birth, life and death of solar systems and galaxies are similar to the biological processes of man, and of the most minute being of creation. As is the macrocosmos, so is the microcosmos. We are a part of the universe, and we may contact it if we so wish.

"There is a third teaching," he added. "All things have their appearance which, to the majority of people, is reality and which is not really so. As the word indicates, they only appear to be so. What is truth? What actually is. What is fallacy? What appears to be. We must rely on these definitions in order to clarify many concepts.

"We divide everything that exists into three kingdoms: animal, vegetable, and mineral, of which, the last we call inert, that is, it has no movement of its own, there is no activity in it. Such is its appearance, but how far we are from reality because there is life in everything; everything moves, everything vibrates. Happily, modern science confirms this assertion everyday. If we learned to vibrate slowly, we would see how all of the particles that compose a rock move, and we would prove that immobility does not exist.

"The same thing happens with our thoughts. If they are positive, they are at a high frequency. On the other hand, the negative ones vibrate slowly. It is the same with sounds and colors; the high and bright ones are of a higher vibration, and the low and dark ones are at a low vibration. You may have observed, for example, that when you are near an angry person, such an emotional state emits bad vibrations that strike your body, and you feel an uneasiness. On the contrary, if the vibrations are a reflection of happiness, you will feel a sense of well-being and peace. I want to point out with this that the vibrations of other beings affect you for better or for worse. The intensity of this effect will be determined by your vibration. It is, therefore, advisable to always have your vibration high so that you will be able to control your own vibrations as well as those of others.

"Matter, mind, and spirit are of different vibratory states of the same Energy, that is, of Him who created us. In matter, we also find differences according to vibration just as we do in mind and in spirit. Within all of them are gradations of vibration according to their evolution. Life in general is a permanent vibration, and therefore, the universe is dynamic. Everything exists through the widely varying manifestation of vibration— from a corpuscle to the stars and galaxies. Naturally, man does not escape this principle. Each individual is made up of diverse vibratory states according to which he will be in harmony or disharmony with himself and others. He will be ill or healthy, ignorant or knowledgeable, alive or dead, spiritual or materialistic, loving or hateful, all of which are merely different levels of the vibration of a mental state.

"As you may see, it is very important to know this principle. Through it, you may modify the vibration and improve mental states, which, if not done, will cause you problems, difficulties, unhappiness, etc. It all depends on you."

At this moment, someone called Nina Soncco, so he got up and left the hut. It must have been something important because he was gone for a while. Upon returning, he continued to talk about another teaching without giving any explanation for his absence.

"When I came this morning, it was raining and I felt cold. Now the sun is shining and I feel hot. These atmospheric changes do not bother me, for each one has its appeal and its beauty. I mention this only to say that everything has its opposites—cold-hot, white-black, positive-negative. That is, they manifest themselves in pairs; they are two aspects, two poles. Cold and hot differentiate themselves from each other only in degrees but they are of the same nature. They are vibrations with a large variation in degrees, up as well as down. Nevertheless, in both extremes, hot and cold exist in some respect. Everything is relative, not absolute. At some point the extremes merge. The same is true with north-south, east-west, light-dark. There is one instant at which the opposites get confused. Where do they begin, and where do they end? Hard and soft, one ends where the other begins.

"I have talked to you about love and hate. Total opposites, but manifestations of the same vibratory mental state. Neither absolute love nor absolute hate exists, but we certainly do feel more love and less hate if we raise ourselves spiritually, or the reverse, we feel more hate if we lower ourselves. Courage and fear are also a pair of opposites that do not escape this principle; in one exists the other. You see how interesting it is to reflect upon all of this," he said with enthusiasm.

"You may always change one mental state for another as long as they are of the same type. For example: hate into love, fear into courage, sickness into health, it depends on your state of consciousness; or, the opposite: love into hate, courage into fear, health into sickness. It will always be possible to realize this change between states of the same kind but of varying vibratory degree.

"Another example will clarify it further. You cannot change a coward into the north or south, but certainly into a brave person, or a lazy one into an active one. This is very important because, with their acceptance, we can achieve desirable mental changes in our enemies, and loved ones. We can make them more positive for the good of everyone. Love is positive, hate is negative; the truth is positive, the lie is negative; the superior thing is positive and the inferior is negative; dignity is positive, pride and vanity are negative. We must avail ourselves of this Principle to be able to carry out mental therapy with optimum results, this I assure you. Can you see how much you can help others just by polarizing situations! By elevating vibrations, with will, you can transform an unpleasant environment into a pleasant one. You can change it with your mere presence, your gaze, your smile, your joy. Your words can help a despairing person and give one hope."

"That is transmutation!" I exclaimed.

"Listen to what I am going to tell you and meditate on it: You can achieve all of this, but first you must learn to alter your own polarity before you can change someone else's."

He became quiet and looked at me seriously. How right he was!

"If you wish to master this, you will have to practice and then you will achieve it. I think you are determined, true?

"A fifth teaching," he added, becoming quiet for a few minutes as if trying to remember something. "On the other hand, it is necessary to remember that everything moves from one side to the other, in one way and then another, goes up and down, moves forward and then back, to the right and then to the left. That is to say, it has a back and forth movement like the waters of a lake. You may have observed that often, without apparent reason, you feel downhearted with no desire to do anything, while at other times, you wake up euphoric, filled with dynamism and the enthusiasm for full activity. What is happening?

"Well, this law functions like all the others. It influences our morale. These laws all act at the same time and affect, in different ways, our bodies in particular and the universe in general. According to this principle, everything comes and goes like a pendulum. First there is oscillation towards one pole, and then towards the other pole. Nothing escapes this principle. One feels it in life itself, in the history of nations that suffer and overcome, that fall and rise. We are born of Inti and we descend; then we die and ascend. This is our most important rhythm—to be born and to die, to inhale and to exhale. The galaxies, the suns, the systems, and the planets are born, reach their maximum expression, then degenerate to their lowest state. They continue in that way, cycle after cycle, only to be reborn again.

"All things repeat themselves; they are born, grow, mature, decay, and die. Everything moves—nothing is at rest. The ocean has its tide that ebbs and flows. Like the others, this Principle guarantees the balanced and harmonious functioning of everything in creation. As long as we do not understand this and cannot use it positively, it will taunt and carry us from one side to the other. We must learn to neutralize and to use it to our benefit so that the actions and reactions are good for us, because it undoubtedly plays a part in creation as well as destruction. Let us make it function like the beating of a heart; the systole and the diastole are beneficial to our life, and they have rhythm.

"Let us get into the sixth teaching," he said. "You know that nothing happens by chance; everything has its origin, its cause, its beginning. Whatever happens afterwards is the effect of that Principle of birth. Your very presence here is due to a cause and the effects of that cause will be subsequent. The effect is future, product of the present, which in a moment will be the past. The thoughts generated by your mind are energy and come out of your head as vibrations, like waves, and return in the future bringing you whatever you have chosen. What I want to tell you is that doing, thinking, acting, and feeling positively will greatly benefit you in the future, which is the effect generated by your mind. When you do something good for someone or speak well of a person, the effect goes out as vibrations of clean colors. Do you know that thoughts have real colors?"

I nodded my head affirmatively.

"Those colors are beautiful and correspondingly attract vibrations of the same color that return, augmented in intensity, through the good that you did or said. See how marvelous! And that is no coincidence. It is an exact law that is called an Immutable Principle, immutable as all of the others of which I have already spoken. If you sow love, you reap love intensified in positive energy. If you sow evil, this vibration will gather more evil along its path, and it will return to you, with additional force, through something unpleasant, such as illness, accident, etc. If you criticize, you will be criticized; if you harm someone, you will be harmed or someone close to you will suffer harm. Everything you sow, which is cause, renders its fruit, which is the effect, that you will reap.

"In general, whatever you sow, good or bad, you will reap amply. It is therefore advisable to offer up in feelings and actions all that this life gives us. If we are bad-tempered, mean, violent, or selfish, we can expect no more than misfortune and bad things in general. Then we complain that God is unfair. How unfair we are with Him! We do not want to admit that we, and not others, are the sole cause of all the ills that plague us, of all the limitations that we suffer, of all the misfortune that comes to us. If you understand this, you can change many things that are harming you, and you will truly have dominion over your life."

After a short pause, Nina Soncco continued, talking about the seventh teaching. "Without a father and a mother, there is no creation—nothing can exist. Everything had its father and mother, masculine and feminine. They exist within every being; gender is merely the external physical difference. In the Hanan Pacha it does not exist. Inti is father-mother, it is Creator, it is Progenitor, it is in everything and it is everything; nothing can exist without it.

"This law has been distorted and misused. People forget that the psychological union of the positive and the negative—masculine with feminine—is the road to generation, to production. One is incapable without the collaboration of the other."

He became quiet because Maria entered the hut to ask him what time we would have lunch. It was already past noon and our meal was getting cold. We got up and followed her in the direction of their hut. It really was late. It was two o'clock! We had not noticed.

Maria and Chaska had already eaten, of course. They served us a very tasty vegetable soup followed by a delicious second dish of jataco with tiny, boiled potatoes accompanied by a small plate of ground, hot pepper. The master generally ate very little, but this time he ate more than usual—perhaps because of the hour or perhaps because the meal was one of his favorites. Once finished, I left immediately. Outside, several people were waiting.

This time, instead of going in the direction of the field, I went down to the edge of the plateau where one could view a river of average flow into which flowed the stream that ran behind my hut. I descended to its bank and sat down on a rock to contemplate the countryside and the crystalline water of the river, which I found to be transparent and unclouded by the mud from the rains. The warmth made me drowsy so I laid down in the shade of a weeping willow (a common and very beautiful tree on those banks) where I fell asleep.

I awoke with the row that the children made as they played around me. They had discovered me and had come down where I was. The sun was already hiding itself behind the mountains as if inviting rest. It was starting to get cool, so I decided to head back. Two of the children took my hands and we climbed up, chatting. They accompanied me to the hut.

That evening I enjoyed a delicious light dinner of corn soup which sat very well in my stomach.

The Fifth Day
Intic Churincuna: The Solar Brotherhood

On the fifth daybreak, I had a beautiful dream; I dreamt of my parents. We were at Samana Wasi in the company of the masters Yupanqui Puma and Nina Soncco, Chaska (being very attentive as always), and her father.

To him I said, "You did not want me to know who you are, but now you see that I do know." He laughed.

The scene changed. It looked like a tunnel. I could hear voices but could not see anybody. We were walking with someone, whom I asked where we were going.

He replied, "To meet you. Now you will see who you are and what you are."

My feet felt very cold. There was excessive humidity. We were practically walking in mud. I awoke to find my feet uncovered.

Five o'clock. A good time to get up. The day was cloudy but with signs of clearing. I prepared a new notebook, put some water on to boil and awaited the arrival of Chaska, who was not long in coming. I told her about my dream.

She said, "Perhaps you will meet him, but it will not be because he seeks you out."

While we were eating breakfast, I thought about her comment. What did she mean? I did not know. Nina

Soncco was already waiting for me, so I went to meet him. He began to talk.

"Almost since the beginning of time, when man began to be conscious of his physical existence, he also started to ask himself questions that he did not understand. So, he decided to get together with others who, like he, were looking for an explanation to their doubts, worries and fears. Thus were born, everywhere on earth, groups of varied numbers of people who, guided by wise, truly enlightened individuals, studied the cosmos and the environment and who looked into themselves and discovered many things.

"That knowledge was jealousy guarded, never being taught openly. They taught only those individuals who showed a real interest and who would make a genuine effort to understand. The majority of people were busy fighting war everywhere, selfishly expanding their dominion, and did not have time to think about these things. On the contrary, they persecuted the people who withdrew from the road of battle and conquest."

"Time passed, and there was an apparent calm, during which time their secrecy continued. Nevertheless, some rulers of empires understood the importance of this knowledge for the ordered life of their nations. They protected these secret groups, and insured their survival. Thus, some rulers were among the first to receive the fundamental nourishment for their spirits. Their initiation into this knowledge necessitated that the governing chiefs do a great deal of preparation (a requisite imposed by the wise men). These heads of state became equitable and just, governing simultaneously as spiritual and temporal rulers of nations that lived happily and in peace. They received the secrets of the knowledge that enlightens, the vibrant spark of initiation.

"Having had the experience of initiation, these chiefs of state insisted that future rulers who would replace them should receive the same preparation so they might also govern with wisdom. The truth was spread throughout the world; one could breathe these teachings in the very air and the winds took charge of carrying it to the confines of the planet.

"In this way, we, too, were fortunate enough to receive that gift from Inti. Our grandparents preoccupied themselves with preserving this knowledge in all of its purity, inculcating the respect and love required to disseminate that knowledge by word of mouth. Their intent was to change us into mystics of the sun. Our Father in the celestial paths and the realm of visible things, is also the visible symbol of the Creator, of that other, dark sun, black, (whom we adepts all know and whose emanation, hidden from our eyes, has a powerful brilliance that we shall someday be able to contemplate because it is inside of us), that sun of the spirit.

"It is within that we must look for it because, if not, we will never find it, no matter how far we search. As I have told you throughout these past few days, each person is a sun that desperately seeks the Great Sun, the light beyond life and death. We are fire, sparks of the flame coated by matter and housed in our heads.

"A sun in miniature will grow until it converts itself into *the god that we carry inside*. Our internal sun will develop. You will have to learn to relate the sun to the Father Creator of all things and the divine sparks to man.

We are *children* of the sun (*Intic Churincuna*). We are its image, its likeness.

"What I am telling you is maintained by the majority of illumined beings in their teachings and, in a veiled form, by the more orthodox churches of today. Man has the duty and the obligation to fight against materialization—against the crystallization of the body—by seeking its purification and liberation. That is to say, he must save his life from among the ruins of his temple and elevate it so that it may occupy its true evolutionary place. Understanding the full magnitude of this, the Great Solar Brotherhood kept this knowledge and these symbolic practices (which, for some, have no importance) because it considered them treasures that man will one day need for his salvation. At this moment there are people making every effort to reach God through a harmonious balance of their thoughts, emotions and actions."

I had previously been told that the Essenes were the first to have the mission of protecting the chalice of spirituality that shines within the world of matter. They were followed by the Gnostics and subsequently, by the Knights Templar, the Rosicrucians and finally, the Masons.

"The lessons with which lived-experiences provide us will be good or bad according to whether or not we are wise—whether we transform them into honey or poison. Some individuals become bitter and negative from their experiences, while others partake of the honey and are positive. Let us permit our spiritual sun to destroy the crystallization of our bodies, and make the eyes that see in the dark, clarify our path once and for all. I am referring to the school of life of our ancestors, which has validity in the present, wherein service and love are daily practices among all of its members. The knowledge upon which we have been reflecting during these past few days comprises truths that the Solar Brotherhood has taught for a long time and we have decided to share this wisdom with you. You have been accepted at your father's request as he is our very beloved brother. We seldom allow this opportunity. We are making an exception with you.

"Once again we are living in times of intolerance and lack of understanding when nothing is respected. You may understand that it is not easy to reveal something that has been preserved with such great love, respect and veneration. We would like to share it with everyone, and it is a shame not to be able to do so."

I felt intense emotions. My heart beat with greater fervor. I could not find words to speak.

Nina Soncco touched my head and continued talking, "Let us make this clear, my son, an initiation is not a ritual or a formula, but a state of mind. Both ritual and formula have their purpose, but the ritualist is mistaken if he believes that rituals and ceremonies alone will ever perfect the human spirit. He is mistaken if he thinks that outer, symbolic degrees will change him into an exceptional person. Ritualism will never elevate a human being above one's own nature. Meditate on this.

"Service also influences the personal and the collective spiritual growth. It is one of the main reasons for our passing through this ephemeral world. It must be totally altruistic, for only then can it be considered service. The helpful person is always ready to please others. By understanding this, we will avoid further disasters on Earth; we shall live in peace, in happiness, seeking mutual assistance just as it was in our past when there existed a humanely just society in which no one lacked what was needed. Service to others is one of the primordial attitudes that strongly unites those who are concerned about the future of humanity and, of course, we all have the capacity to serve.

Why is it not effected? Do you know why it is not done? It is not because we fail to recognize the need, but rather, because it is more comfortable not to do it, and we are completely occupied in our own selfish interests. Opportunities to serve pass before our very eyes without our seeing them. They pass like the water in the stream which we think is all the same but which is never the same. We should take advantage of every opportunity that presents itself in order to live as one who serves, fully enjoying life without selfishness, or rancor, or vengeance. With hate, we cannot build anything good. We should avoid the ambitions that are the cause of all wars. In the past the conquerors did a great deal of damage to us by destroying our culture, and it is happening again today."

Did he refer to the extremists who zealously seek political careers in the world market for their own egotistic purposes?

"Nevertheless, we should not continue to ruminate on these horrible episodes. Let us build a more just society that is conscious of its mission, and that will not allow man to continue making such mistakes. Because of our origin, all beings who inhabit this vast universe are brothers and sisters; we must understand and assimilate this in order to live in peace. If not, our attitudes will again produce imbalance and disharmony on Earth; Earth will continue shaking herself with greater violence in an attempt to reach physical and energetic stability. Speaking as we are of the Earth, I should tell you that there are three realms, planes or levels that we must know and traverse: *Kay Pacha* is the earth on which we live and which we hardly know even superficially; *Ajay Pacha* or the realm of above or beyond; and *Uju Pacha* or the realm of below."

Perhaps he referred symbolically to heaven, purgatory, and the hell of some religions, or to the Inti unmanifest, the Inti revealed, and the Inti transcending its physical covering? Perhaps he meant the existence of Inti's physical, psychic and spiritual identities? Or, he may have alluded to the physical, astral and mental bodies.

He looked at me with a roguish smile as if divining my thoughts and said, "Yes, it is all of that and much more. We will expand on this at another time. What I now want to tell you is that man is his own sculptor. It is what he thinks of himself that will mold his physical aspect, giving it beauty or ugliness. If, within himself, he is young, then so shall he be on the outside. Do not forget that eternity has no old age. If there is activity internally, it will be noted externally. On the other hand, if all activities cease deep inside, old age will begin to set in on the surface and the disintegration of the body will take place. Life depends on the understanding of and obedience to the cosmic laws which govern everything. That is to say, in just such a conscious way,

80

we shall be able to see the cause behind all manifestation.

"This is the Solar Brotherhood to which you will belong in a few more days. Its philosophy is contained in the teachings of these days.

"The true mystic grows in light and beauty. In one's philosophy there is no room for mediocrity, pedantry, narrow-mindedness, and pretension. Make all knowledge an intimate experience for yourself, because that is what is real. Find balance and you will find the joy of living and of equilibrium. Distrust extremes, for all I have already told you, they are dangerous.

"For thousands of years, myths and legends have existed—a popular wisdom, a camouflaged truth, a reality that kept us in balance with the cosmos. As a result, our education was more effective and not as it is nowadays, via books which fill our brains but only our brains. So it is that the personality is limited and rebellious, always constituting the real obstacle to our advancement."

"It is necessary to spiritualize matter and thought because we are sinking under the weight of ideas and of a culture that has become solely intellectual and verbal. Get closer to your real source and do not mimic others because you run the risk of destroying your creative spiritual powers while seeking affirmation from a false individualism. Go in search of the light which is daughter to the truth, to the sun. Contemplate the physical light but do not lose sight of the other Dark Light which is the only one that will allow you to see in the darkness, with an intense brilliance in the middle of the night, with rays of knowledge giving you life. With the Light you will grow.

"I have spoken to you before now about the Light. One finds the truth in solitude, in the plenitude of silence, in a search truly individual, on a path solely yours where reason does not interfere. When reason is quiet and the concepts and the words become empty and disappear, truth shines through in fullness because language may either steer us onto the correct path or distance us from it. It is time now to unlearn in order to know because at present, man has dissociated himself from a society that has become his mortal enemy, alienating him.

"All of what I am telling you needs to be taught, and taught by example if it is to be believed. We must become servants of humanity. If we want others to follow us, we must be true leaders; otherwise, others will have every right to doubt our sincerity.

"Let us make them judge us by the fruit of our labors, that is, let us talk little and serve more, with great love. Let us not be fiery preachers, for there are already enough of them on the planet—people who talk about the damage that drugs do, all the while having some between their fingers and blowing the smoke into you face, and others who warn that alcohol is bad for your health while they themselves drink. Many speak of morality which they do not know and of rectitude which they do not practice. Others wish to be ascetics and go off to the mountains; they want to go where no one contradicts, hurts or opposes them, in order to maintain their imagined balance and purity; they do not care to serve anyone or bother to work among other people. Ironically, self-mastery and spiritual aspiration can only be attained in such an environment; in no other way will we gain experience or learn anything. Finally, there are people who believe that, by ceasing to ingest certain foods, they are advancing. It is of no avail if we are nourishing our bodies with nectar and ambrosia,[26] when the mind is an ossuary replete with dark thoughts or, rather, white sepulchers: beautiful to contemplate from the outside and on the inside, full of nauseous stenches.

"We must ask ourselves what thoughts we have in our minds and what is our mental nourishment. A negative mental situation can be easily maintained, and even more so in the solitude of the mountains, but it is not at all constructive. An idle mind is the devil's workshop, as they very accurately say. The most certain path to internal purity and cleanliness of heart is to be occupied all day with focusing our wishes, feelings, and emotions towards the practical problems of life, and working for the good of all. We must be right there helping the needy and the poor who need it, extending our love not only to our families, but also, to the families of others as if they were our brothers and sisters.

"Universal brotherhood will be a reality when individual love is not confined only to our family. We have to learn to be universal and to love everyone from whatever place in life we happen to be stationed. This is our true work and the only path that leads to real excellence, our evolution and our growth. I am certain that the Solar Brotherhood has the means and, therefore, the hope of achieving these ends."

The Sixth Day
Samana Wasi

For the first time in six days, I did not sleep well. I was restless and tense. At three in the morning, I looked at my watch for the last time so I must have slept about three hours—no more.

As on all of the previous evenings, I had eaten with Chaska the night before. Once alone and in bed, I tried to organize my ideas. I could not help thinking about the Solar Brotherhood—a school of life as Nina Soncco called it—which I would come to know intimately thanks to my father. I could not fall asleep until dawn, at which time my ramblings continued in another dimension while my body rested.

I have the not-so-conscious impression of having been in a strange place with a pleasant environment. It looked like an underground gallery where there were people dressed in clothing different from everyday wear. It was very beautiful. I was impressed by the color and shape. All of a sudden the gallery transformed into a room whose walls were made of finely worked stones like the ones seen in the Temple of the Sun, Koricancha, in Cusco. A moment later, the clothing was no longer visible—just the faces of the people, who moved close to me then farther away, moving their lips although I could hear nothing. One of the faces came close and I felt arms holding me by the shoulders and shaking me. I could not breathe for the fear. I was suffocating. I awoke with a startle to find Chaska shaking me. I do not know how this interesting dream would have proceeded.

I got up still tired. While I washed myself, Chaska prepared breakfast. We shared coffee, a delicious corn pancake and a brief conversation. She told me that we would also have lunch together as there was to be no dinner for me that evening nor any food at all the following day, by order of Nina Soncco. This caught my attention and surprised me, but as usual, I did not have a chance to ask about the order, and Chaska offered no explanation. She left, and I went out behind her in the direction of the master's hut. He had affectionately called me "Son" the previous day; it was a gesture that touched me deeply.

Nina Soncco received me with great fondness. I felt the warmth of his heart and the love that he radiated for everyone and everything. His interest in continuing my instruction was noticeable in all of his gestures.

"Thank you, God," I said silently, "for this opportunity which continues to be like a dream for me!"

"Today is the second to the last day that you are with us," he said solemnly.

I interrupted him to ask for the nth time that he allow me to stay and live with them. This time his reply was an even more final "No!" I should go back to take care of my daily responsibilities and to get started on others. I was to get them straightened out in the shortest time possible.

In an almost pleading way, I tried a different approach. "In any case, please allow me to return when you think it convenient."

"Perhaps," he answered. "Nevertheless, it will be when we call you. You will have to wait for us without any commitment on our part." And then, he continued where he had left off earlier.

"Today I have to talk to you about a project that is not only interesting as an experience, but is also very important and of urgent need. It is a suggestion and nothing else. You are free to accept it or not. The project has the name *Samana Wasi*.[27] This house of physical, psychic, and spiritual health will have to be dedicated to the unselfish service of the most needy people. If you accept, it will be part of your work in the Sacred Valley of the Incas."

For an instant he was quiet as he studied me.

"I accept," I said. "Your suggestions are loving orders for me, and I receive them with the same love with which you give them. I will do everything I can so that this idea may materialize as soon as possible. I am very happy to carry out this mission."

He smiled.

"You will have to choose the appropriate site very carefully. It will not be easy, for in every project aimed at the good of society, there are more difficulties than in any other kind of endeavor. Undoubtedly you will not be able to accomplish this alone. You will have to call upon people of goodwill and charitable heart who wish to make the idea a reality, and who will help it materialize through concrete action. For now, I think you already have enough information to undertake this work and to prepare all of those who will collaborate with you.

"The admirable community of our ancestors was based on three governing rules: truth, honor, work.[28] Its socio-economic center was in the ayllu—or village—supported by two labor institutions—the *Aini*[29] and the *Minca.*[30] These concepts and the wisdom I received from the Solar Brotherhood inspired this idea which I now suggest to you. There will be no racial, religious or political discrimination in it. All beings of goodwill on earth who wish to help our needy brothers and sisters will be welcomed.

"You will build Samana Wasi on three important pillars of life:

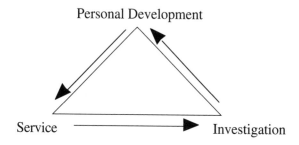

Personal Development

Service → Investigation

"Service, because essentially, as I told you earlier, life has to be that of mutual assistance. It is with this understanding that Samana Wasi will be concerned with attention to all of the needy, and particularly, to the abandoned children and the destitute elderly—the two most neglected and forgotten extremes of this fleeting existence which unfolds on this planet. In our Nation, there are, as in many parts of the world, thousands of homeless children who live in the streets with all of the unforeseeable consequences, or those who are living at home but are poorly educated because of economic difficulties or the ignorance of their parents who themselves need to be rehabilitated, for their own sakes and that of society. It is necessary to restore these children's confidence in the future, the dignity that they lost, and the psycho-physical equilibrium they need in order to live in harmony with themselves. In this way, we shall achieve a different society whose citizens are free from anger, hate or other traumas. Not by giving harsh criticism and turning our backs on them can we adequately guide those who are beginning to live their lives. Neither are threats and punishments the appropriate means. Rather, we all must view their problems with magnanimity, taking an interest in their lives, feeling their needs, desires, and pleasures, and trying to create a family around them. That great family that will perhaps achieve the miracle of making these children a little more mature and the older folks a little youthful.

"And, speaking of the seniors, it is also necessary to recuperate the elderly who have the experience of an entire life. Return to them the will to live fully until the end of their days, and give them the confidence and the security that they need to feel useful to humanity. Each one of them has something to teach us; the elderly are not novices in the art of life.

"Although it is true that from the moment of birth, we begin to die physically, it is not good that we live mentally planning for death under the pretext of providing for the future. From the beginning, we prepare ourselves for the future. Having studied or worked, we all look for some economic security which is normal, but we spend our lives accumulating wealth for the future. When we finally realize this (if we get that far), we are already old and we have done nothing constructive for ourselves. Then, we look towards retirement, reflecting more or less in the following way: 'I have already done my duty. My children are successful, or at least, they are independent. I no longer have obligations to anyone. I will enjoy my retirement while waiting to die because no one needs me anymore.'

"I ask myself if it is worthwhile living like that. And, as if that were not enough, their children do everything possible to make them feel totally useless and a family burden, by preventing them from doing what they want. Mistreatment and thoughtlessness are what the old folks receive from children who forget that they, too, in the not too distant future (life of Earth is very short) will receive the same treatment if their attitude does not change. Hence, they in turn will await death because they will feel themselves equally a burden. It must be very sad to feel such loneliness! That is not life! Life must be lived fully each day. We must enjoy every moment of our work and of our times of rest. We have come here to be happy, and we must achieve this by not allowing obstacles to dishearten us, and by allowing the difficulties encountered in our path to become experiences for our continued growth. We shall consciously achieve this attitude by seriously meditating on the following questions:

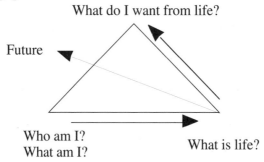

What do I want from life?

Future

Who am I?
What am I?

What is life?

89

"When we have come to understand in some way, when we have even a vague idea about these three unknowns, which appear easy to answer. Then we shall be able to properly orient our lives in the right direction, for some field of human endeavor. We shall know what we really are. It is therefore fundamental to remember and respect human dignity. The old folks, like the children, are our future.

"Investigation is important because it is necessary to recover and become familiar with the cosmological and cosmogonic Quechua tradition in order to have a greater understanding of our past and present realities, and their projection for the future. Our race has lost contact with traditions and no longer knows anything of its ancestors. It ignores what it was and assimilates new ways of life with great difficulty. Given the circumstances in which we now live, it is necessary to understand other schools of life that exist in other countries and continents. In the same way, we need to recover and become knowledgeable of medicinal remedies used by our forefathers for the good health of the people. Native and foreign medicinal plants as well as medicinal practices from the past, present and future will need to be used in whatever way possible. Preventive medicine will continue to be the best. Similarly, agricultural research will be another area whose end it will be to achieve more and better natural foods, recovering native species of great nutritional value as alternatives to improve our diet."

"In short, we need to research and assimilate everything that is good for us all. We need to seek with humility, to move from ignorance into knowledge in order to acquire wisdom. Let us not forget that the five senses discover and experiment. Understanding is the faculty of acquiring knowledge as the basis for wisdom, which must be accompanied by a manifestation and expression in practice and work. Knowledge, like wisdom, should be used to serve. Wisdom is the unfolding of life within form, that is, it is the intuitive assimilation of truth. We must reach this state of consciousness.

"Personal Growth is vital because all of those who freely and consciously become a part of Samana Wasi to help by serving the needy, will, at some determined moment, have to look at and ask themselves questions like: What am I? Do I really know who I am? Am I this physical body or something else? They will also have to ask themselves what they think life is. Is it that lapse of fifty, seventy or one hundred years and nothing more? Or, does life have a greater dimension? They will have to learn. The opportunity to grow spiritually will be given through practices, attitudes and exercises that will awaken their dormant faculties in order to work in harmony and in balance for the good of humanity. This personal development is very important."

"Samana Wasi will be a place where the person in need finds peace, tranquility and understanding so that, after one's psycho-physical recuperation, one may return to daily activities with another mentality: that of service to others. Besides attending to children and to the elderly who are its reason for existence, Samana Wasi will also need to be concerned with receiving people who, because of nervous tensions resulting from their environment, are on the edge of psychic and consequently, physical disequilibrium. These brothers and sisters will need the support of Samana Wasi to recover their stability.

"Many individuals suffer because they do not understand what is happening to them or around them. They blow their problems up out of proportion and place too much value on their feelings which results in despair, followed by obsession. They end up being completely disturbed, which is unfair to them and to their loved ones. Such persons need the warmth of an environment where they are received with much love and concern. The place will have to be Samana Wasi where one may forget one's difficulties and learn to think first about one's own healing, which is certainly a most important concern in life. Much good can be accomplished after this.

"The first priority is one's life and health. Without these, the individual cannot take care of or resolve what is beyond oneself. I am certain that from that beginning a new person will emerge without limits, dedicated to good works and to teaching by example. Of greater value is one person who acts than one million people who feel and talk. To feel and talk is of no advantage if it fails to promote action. This is a mission that must be made real for the good of everyone. It, too, should grow without boundaries of any kind. The details of its organization and its support are yours to resolve. It will not be easy, but you will have to do it.

"Now, go have lunch and prepare for tomorrow. It will be your last day among us and your first in a new concept of life. Regardless, you will leave, taking with you experience and knowledge about which you will be able to talk and write with great caution. There are truths that you will not yet mention because they may be misinterpreted, causing problems instead of benefits."

I left, but not before thanking him once again for his great kindness. Considerate as always, Chaska was waiting for me so that we might eat together. During the meal I became so engrossed in thought, that we finished eating before I realized we had not spoken throughout the entire meal. Afterwards, Chaska laughed loudly. I asked her to forgive my absent demeanor.

Understanding, she said, "Do not worry. The same thing happens to me—especially after listening to Nina Soncco or my father."

Taking advantage of the moment, I questioned her about the latter but, as on previous occasions, I received no answer. As if she had not heard me, she spoke, making reference to the last moments that we were spending together since, as I was not going to be eating again, we would not be sharing any more occasions like this together.

For the first time, I realized the nearness of my departure, and I felt a great sadness. I accompanied Chaska to the creek where she always washed the dishes, and I helped her put everything away in a basket. When I asked her whether or not I would see her on the day of my departure, she told me that I would, in spite of the early hour.

I was left alone. I had not felt lonely or sad during those days, which had neither time nor space for me until then. They were days in an eternal, endless dream, a dream which now seemed to have reached an end. I had the sensation of having lived there always, and that I would leave, entering a new world foreign to me.

How would I react when I had to say good-bye to Nina Soncco, Maria, Chaska, and the others who might be there at my departure? What exactly should I say to Nina Soncco, the master? Insist, perhaps, that he allow me to stay and live with them? I loved them all as if they were part of my family and, in truth, they were. I think that finally I had learned to love everyone and everything, but given the circumstances, I did not feel happy. I did not worry whether or not people would believe what I had experienced. I simply felt sorrow for all that I was going to leave. At one point during my stay, Nina Soncco had alluded to this very moment.

"Do only that which you are doing. Do not run away from the present moment; live with a receptive mind, instant to instant, and then seek your place in the universe," he had told me.

I meditated on these thoughts during the hours that remained, but I continued to feel sad, sorrowful and anxious. I tried to find some peace by taking a walk with no particular direction in mind. Unhurriedly, I walked up and down nearby hills. The day was ending. What a beautiful sunset! In the silence of the sunset, I could hear my heartbeat, accelerated by the effort of my walk.

Back inside the hut, I cleaned up a little. Outside a cold wind was blowing. I lay in bed thinking about a myriad of things. Somehow, I felt slightly more encouraged. I was sleepy, so I covered up with my poncho. I did not need anything more. The air was warm, there was a fire in the hearth, and I fell fast asleep.

The Seventh Day
Initiation

It was as beautiful a day as all the rest that I had spent in this small, almost unnoticeable Andean village. I felt happiness and, at the same time, sadness as it was the last day I would be spending in the company of Nina Soncco—wise and humble farmer, extraordinary man, and exceptional and true teacher; his mere presence inspired respect, veneration and much love. He appeared to be frail because of his age, but he became a marvel of energy and strength when he began to talk. He virtually lit up and was transformed into a giant of the mysterious Andes.

Those ancient mountains seemed to be symbolized by Soncco and my experiences in this village. Incredible wonders must be hidden in the caverns and hidden canyons of the Andes! Unfathomable treasures of spirit were mine to only glimpse during this week of pilgrimage.

On more than one occasion, I had asked Nina Soncco for permission to live with him. His negative answer on the previous day had been definite, so I knew that I must leave.

On that final morning I ate no breakfast, neither did I eat the night before. I was not hungry, anyway, but I did feel uneasy. I had the feeling that something more significant than on all the other days was about to occur. The past seven days would be engraved in my heart and in my memory forever. I thought that I might be prepared for the final encounter; at least, I had done everything that the master had instructed. So, I continued to meditate until he called me.

What a surprise! At six o'clock, Chaska, whom I did not expect to see again until the time of my departure, entered. She had brought some tea that Nina Soncco had ordered I should drink. Of what herb was it made? I had no idea, but it was sweet-smelling and tasty. She told me that the master was expecting me in his hut at seven o'clock, which would be in one hour.

I drank the tea, and arranged my things. With my notebook in hand, I left the hut and went to the door to observe, perhaps for the last time, the small plaza with its large old ceiba tree at the center. The village was still sleeping; the silent huts looked like stationary sentries awaiting some order. I could hear the murmur of the little stream, where I had washed daily, and where I had played on more than one occasion with the children of the village.

I felt a certain nostalgia so I retraced my footsteps to tell Chaska ñahui that these were indeed the final moments we would spend together. I thanked her sincerely for everything that she had so lovingly done to make my stay even more pleasant. She smiled with that smile that had become so familiar. Her enormous black eyes, bright as stars, looked affectionately at me. She told me that we would probably see one another that night but more likely, at dawn the following day before I left. She departed without saying good-bye, but when she reached the plaza, she called in a voice loud enough for me to hear.

"We will be together again tonight."

The wait seemed long with minutes passing slowly. I thought that seven o'clock would never come, so to hasten the time, I decided to walk very slowly toward my teacher's hut which I would probably enter for the last time. But the hut was too close, so I waited a few meters from the door.

I heard voices inside which meant that Nina Soncco was not alone. As if my arrival had been sensed inside, one of the men came out. I did not recognize him. He was approximately my height and about fifty years old, with gray hair (a rarity in these people). Having answered my greeting, he invited me to enter the hut.

Inside with Nina Soncco were seven other men, all of whom responded to my greeting with a smile. Two of them took me by my arms, and the Gray-Haired One spoke to me.

"Today is a very important and special occasion for you."

It was the seventh day of the first month of the year, and will always be an unforgettable date for me. With the authorization and permission of Nina Soncco, Illac Uma of the Solar Brotherhood, and by request of my father, I was about to be accepted and received as an active member of this community known as The Children of the Sun.

Everything began so swiftly that I had no time to react. I was deeply moved as I heard my father's name, and longed for his presence. I could not breathe. I had a knot in my throat.

Realizing my predicament, Nina Soncco came over to me and took my notebook saying, "You will not need this." With an embrace he calmed me down.

He then invited me to take a seat at his side on a bench situated in front of his bed. Next, something truly astonishing happened—something that made me think once again that I was living a fantasy. The men pushed back the master's bed, and removed some sheep skins that were underneath it covering an underground entrance to some place unknown. Immediately the Gray-Haired One blindfolded my eyes with a violet cloth native to this village. He ordered me to stoop down.

I then seemed to descend down some moist, slippery, earthen steps. I was being held tightly by my arms. We began to walk very slowly. The air was damp. We passed a place where there was a lot of water. My feet got wet. At some point it seemed to be raining. We walked a little farther, then my escorts had me sit down on a rock. My feet were soaked because we had walked a long way on muddy ground. They left me alone in a silence that seemed unending.

Suddenly, I heard a voice that asked loudly, "What are you?"

These words resounded in what seemed to be an echo chamber. I sensed footsteps which slowly diminished in the distance. Almost immediately I heard another voice as loud as the previous one. "Who are you?"

The voice disappeared without an echo. It's owner seemed to be running.

Again, silence. What am I? Who am I? Silently, I repeated these questions. Did I really know what or who I was? The answer seemed obvious, very simple; nevertheless, I could not reply because the answer was not exactly as I had supposed. I needed to reflect on it more carefully. Again, another loud voice suddenly shook me with another question.

"What is life… f…f…f?"

The voice echoed and faded slowly as if moving away, only to return abruptly and with more power.

"What do you expect of life?"

The reverberating voice stopped suddenly into silence.

A few seconds later, the whispers of several distant voices softly but insistently repeated, "Investigate, search, be kind, help, serve, and you will grow." The voices continued their urging.

Then the rock on which I was sitting moved violently, and I fell flat on my face, for I couldn't see through the blindfold to reach for a support. I braced my hands on the muddy ground to stand up, but at that moment I felt two strong arms that lifted me up and practically dragged me several meters. They washed my hands then sat me on a rock; whether it was the same rock or another one, I couldn't tell. I had the impression that they had left and that I was alone.

I reached out my hands in the hope finding something that would at least give me some idea of where I was.

A horrendous shiver went through my body! I had touched a cold hand, seemingly lifeless, and frozen to the spot! After calming down somewhat, I realized that it was the body of a person lying on a huge, table-like rock. I made my way around it. When I could not find another rock on which to sit, I was tempted to remove the blindfold. At that moment, someone helped me to sit down.

The initiatory ritual continued. Many strangely beautiful things took place which I cannot relate to you now.

Afterwards, my clothes and the blindfold were removed. I was shown to an exit through which I could go to bathe myself. I passed through it to encounter another of many surprises. There was the river that I had visited a few days earlier, located at the south end of the village and the plain. This made me think that the tunnel was quite long.

I finished bathing, and turned back to the cave, but I couldn't find the mouth of the cavern through which I had just walked! It was about three or four o'clock in the afternoon, for the sun was at about forty-five degrees to the west. Anxiously, I searched again and again. There was some vegetation, but not enough to hide an entrance. Besides, when I had come out, I had noticed that the opening was very wide. Finally, I looked toward the river in an effort to get my bearings and some sense of direction. When I turned toward the plateau, I found myself face to face with two friendly farmers whom I did not know.

Once again the blindfold covered my eyes, and I permitted myself to be led. I was getting chilled, being naked and wet. They put sandals on me and a kind of blanket that draped over my back. As we continued walking, the air temperature became more and more pleasant until I felt warm. We stopped for a few moments. Silence.

The blanket and blindfold were removed. During some moments of silence, I was dressed in very beautiful attire.

What a spectacle to behold! I thought we had gone back a hundred or a thousand years! There were twelve men, among them the Gray-Haired One. The garments worn by Nina Soncco were most impressive and made him look taller. All of the men were dressed in shiny clothing of bright colors.

Between Nina Soncco and me there was a strange-looking altar with a carved, pointed stone approximately one and a half meters high. The detail of its angles and lines reminded me of some that I had seen in Pisac and Ollantaytambo. The top part was shaped like a pyramid, which rested on a cube, which in turn rested on another cube; the entire altar was carved in reddish stone. What a beauty! The apex of the pyramid supported, with a type of bracket, something similar to a small, deep bowl of shiny, yellow metal—perhaps gold. In it, charcoal burned to produce a blue, transparent flame. Around the altar were four, wooden pillars driven into the ground and standing about a meter high. A receptacle rested atop each pillar; a wood burning flame in each receptacle. There appeared to be no smoke, or else it was escaping through air shafts which I could not discern.

When my robes were all arranged, Nina Soncco said, "Place you left hand over the fire on the altar."

I did so. The Gray-Haired One began to say something which I initially did not understand. Then his voice became clearer and resounded in my head.

My escorts were all holding hands around the altar. It seemed as if they were circling, and intoning a mantric melody that began to gather form and strength. My entire body was vibrating. Although my surroundings remained visible, they became transparent and I no longer perceived them as they were, for they seemed to symbolize something else.

In reality, what I saw was an energy—the singular force that permeates all things. For me this was a definite, concrete revelation of the universal unity in the force that, until now, I had grasped only in my intellect. This force suddenly penetrated my life as a true experience, as something more than words, as a live substance that filled me to the extremes. It is to experience that state beyond words (although words describe its substance, they fail to convey the meaning). The smallest animal is moved by the same unknown energy that moves me.

I could see myself, but I seemed to have fled my own body! There was a brilliant light! What was it? A luminosity completely lacking in form filled my vision. Then, everything changed in its appearance; it became a moment in time that no longer exists, or never existed—it was a time without age. I believe it was a return to the origins.

(Looking for you during much of my life, I found my real self. It is to be fully the essence of one's self. Wisdom concerns only the I, and knowledge the *not-I*. Archaic teaching is accurate in essence although it has been discounted in interpretation.)

I heard a distant voice telling me, "When you awaken, you will realize that this was all a dream. There are superior laws that govern our experiences. They show us the path of giving, of love and of genuine concern for others, and not the path of acquisition. If they so desire, men and women may travel this path together, but realization is very individual."

I do not know whether I heard these reflections and thoughts or whether my mind created them. The only thing for certain is that when I returned to my senses, I was stretched out on a black, thickly woven, Incan blanket, placed on an enormous stone carved in the shape of a table. Beside me on another stone table, lying on a bed of wild flowers, was the corpse of another man (initially, I had thought that he was going through the same trance-like states). I could not distinguish his features clearly, as he was lying five or six meters away in the dim light of one of the fires.

I remained in that same position waiting for someone to arrive. It was not long before the Gray-Haired One appeared. He helped me to get up and asked me how I felt.

"Very well," I told him, "but surprised and confused about everything I am experiencing."

At that moment, Nina Soncco entered in the company of ten more men who were beautifully attired in impressive garments. Their clothes seemed to be decorated in gold, because every time the men moved, they would glimmer, emitting rays of light in all directions. They arranged themselves around the table on which the other man was laid. The Gray-Haired One took my left arm, and led me to the right side of the master. I looked at the man lying before me. He was certainly dead and yet, he looked familiar. With noticeable solemnity and emotion, Nina Soncco, Illac Uma of the Solar Brotherhood, said, "Many years have passed since the death of our master, Amaru Yupanqui Puma, but, nevertheless, his teachings become increasingly relevant."

I could not believe, nor did I want to accept what was going through my mind at that moment! I was about to collapse when I was caught by the arms. It could not be! It was Yupanqui Puma! The same person I had seen nearly forty years earlier!

"But this is impossible," I said aloud, because I could no longer contain myself. Nina Soncco looked at me with understanding and acceptance.

"It is possible for us, who know the art of preservation. We shall continue to conserve his body for a great deal longer. He was the most important and the last of the truly enlightened ones that we knew. In addition, he was a direct descendant of the Incas; they are little understood in the history of our nation, because they were so spiritually evolved. Those who see him are the ones whom we accept and allow to become part of the Solar Brotherhood."

Once again they all held hands, including me in the circle. One of them began to whisper softly some words which I recognized and which we all repeated.

"I. a...N. K.[31]*"*

I felt something like an electric current throughout my body. It seemed to enter through my left hand and to leave through my right hand after having passed through my spinal column.

The ceremonial meeting continued with additional surprises for an undetermined length of time.

At the conclusion, they took off the beautiful garments in which they had dressed me, replacing them with my own. Once more I was blindfolded, and we began to walk back through the same damp passages, until we climbed the steps under Nina Soncco's bed and hut.

I had grown to love this teacher, the Illac Uma, as if he were my own father. At that moment, I understood the tears of my father at the death of Yupanqui Puma. My blindfold was removed for the last time, and I found myself in the company of Nina Soncco and the original six men, as if nothing extraordinary had happened. Some of the men were standing while the master was seated on the bench in front of his bed. Everything was just as it had been at the beginning of the day.It was already evening. Once again, Nina Soncco invited me to sit next to him while the others leisurely came and went from the hut.

After a short time, the Gray-Haired One asked me to follow him as he went in the direction of the village plaza. The evening was adorned with stars, and the air was not cold. We stopped in front of the ceiba tree. Within a few moments, the others arrived with Nina Soncco who sat down on the grass. The rest of us did the same, forming a circle.

The master then gifted me with a beautiful speech, insistently reminding me of the responsibility I had accepted and of my assignment of Samana Wasi. I thanked him for his words, and the others for their companionship and assistance during that last day. Once more, I expressed my deepest gratitude for the opportunity offered to me and the high honor that I had been given.

I was one of them! How exciting! Until that moment; I had not realized that Chaska was with us. I was very happy to see her. With a smile she handed me a bowl of hot tea, or at least, that is what I thought it was. It was most welcome after having an empty stomach for so long. I asked Nina Soncco for his permission before I drank. The liquid had a somewhat bitter taste, almost oily, and it made me nauseous. I had to control myself to finish it little by little, as I supposed that I should.

I remember nothing else as I fell backward. I felt arms catching me by the shoulders and laying me on the grass.

Then I got up without any difficulty—without realizing it, I had already stood up, but I was weightless. I could see my body lying on the grass! I began to levitate! I was frightened, but at the same time, I was aware that other people were there caring for me. I heard a voice of encouragement, and I saw many sights of indescribable beauty. The colors were alive, and they moved. Everything was alive! Well, that is how it was.

Unlike the previous mornings, it was Nina Soncco himself who woke me the following day. I was in my bed! I suppose that they had left me there the previous night. I went outside to clean up; I could still see the last stars that bid farewell to the night and give way to a new dawn. For me, it was the beginning of a new life!

"My son," said Nina Soncco, noticeably moved, "you have to leave today, and it is possible that we shall not see one another again. You must not return unless we call you. At any rate, you will receive news from us whenever it is necessary. You will always be present in our thoughts, and you already have a place in our hearts. We shall support you in all of your activities. In whatever circumstance you may find yourself, maintain constant balance, harmony and peace within you no matter how difficult this may be. Only from your center can you be just and fair.

"Your life will not be easy now, just as it was not in the past. You will not be understood; in fact, people will vituperate against you. Seek people who are genuine—not those who appear good, or those who sell themselves for a better position or for more comfort.

"You will find friends—those who can truly love. When you make a mistake, they will help you to overcome it by helping you see the error; they will protect your reputation when you are absent. Such people will always be necessary to any activity related to the good of others.

"You are our youngest brother; you know now what you have to do. Speak with caution, tact and without offense to anyone. Basically, speak only when you have something to say, something that will be of benefit to others. Act with humility and with fairness so that any teaching also becomes a lesson for you. Example is the best teacher of all.

"Remember that there are universal laws that govern everything and forgive nothing. The effect is always a consequence of a cause. It is the time for positive attitudes, for decision making, and for action. No longer is it the time for theories. Man has intellectualized too much in the belief that thinking is the best course, while what is best is to act, not just to think and to feel. Do not forget, either, that your brothers and sisters are spread out all over the face of the earth, and each of them must be served equally."

He hugged me with great affection, with all the warmth expressed by his name. Maria, having arrived unnoticed with Chaska, did the same.

The sun was rising. We left the hut. There was a need for air to breathe.

Outside, José Pumaccahua stood next to a saddled horse. I had not seen him since the first day. We exchanged greetings. I hugged Chaska who, in return, kissed me on the cheek. She had been extremely good to me; all of them had.

"My father was with you yesterday," she told me unexpectedly.

"The one with the gray hair?" I asked curiously.

"Yes," she replied tersely. She became silent, for she was crying. I thanked her for that last piece of information and I kissed her. Unfortunately, I had not observed the Gray-Haired One more diligently. He would some day replace Nina Soncco! He was the future Illac Uma!

We left, walking back to that other world, yanking the reluctant horse by its reins. I could not see the way; my tears would not allow me. With great sorrow, I left that small, beautiful, and strange village that had filled me with life throughout those seven days.

The higher up the mountain we climbed, the more beautiful the village looked; it also seemed more distant, as if the village were moving away, making sure that I couldn't reach it. We went over the mountain crest with its small, resting places, carved from the rocks. From then on, the village was hidden from view. Who knows if I will ever see it again.

Rivers, narrow passes, mountains, and beautiful landscapes greeted me as we made our way back to my home. We did not talk at all. Words were not necessary. My mind and my heart had remained behind. Besides, José's gestures were enough in themselves. In certain places that he considered necessary, he would cover my lowered head with that familiar piece of black cloth (I supposed that it was the same one as before). On this trip, however, he did offer a short explanation:

"I am covering your eyes so that you are not tempted to return unless we call you."

Maybe he was right. The trip lasted an extra day in order to further disorient me.

"I am sorry," continued José, "but those are Nina Soncco's orders. We all are human, and we make mistakes. Therefore, we must be sure that everything ends well and without problems. You will have to learn to wait patiently."

So it was that I was led groping along paths which only Pumaccahua knew. He would take off my blindfolds for periods of rest, eating, or sleeping under huge boulders or in caves. He was always careful that certain spots would not be overtly visible as landmarks. Our return journey was not only slow, but also dangerous. On many occasions, we passed through places so narrow that we had to follow one behind the other practically stretched out on the ground. At other times, we walked through rivers. I do not know for certain if all of this was deliberate, but I am certain that the trip took us four and a half days.

We arrived at Chupani just as the sun was directly overhead. This was our last stop, and we were exhausted, so we used lunch time as an excuse for taking a rest. Also, I think it was a good pretext for spending a little more time together.

The mountains looked different to me: the Tantanmarca and the Kuntur Sencca looked even higher, while the Tacllancca and the Pujcru had rolled their summits down until they blended with the plain. The Pachac and Sutoc Rivers which lovingly protect the Chupani plateau, gave the impression that they carried some kind of a competitive energy in their bubbling, crystalline waters. These energized streams form the Pumahuanca, which is a river of life to the flora, fauna and people who inhabit its shores.

Finally, the dreaded moment arrived when José Pumaccahua—my last and only remaining link to the village—had to begin his journey back to the mountains. José was in a hurry, and he declined to rest for even a day before starting out again. He hugged me warmly with that special embrace reserved for family and friends; it was the same manner in which the farmers embraced my father. I returned his hug with a great deal of emotion, and thanked him for his kindness. I assured him that I would never forget him. He was a man of few words, but when he wanted to express his feelings, he did so with such openness that anyone could sense his sincerity.

I watched him leading his horse up the hill (neither of us had ridden that horse on the return trip). He would disappear and then reappear as he wended through the vegetation and the undulations of Chupani's rolling countryside. He traveled beyond my sight as he went behind the Korihuayrachina. I climbed up onto a large rock to catch a final glimpse of him, but he was gone.

Alone I set out on the last leg of my return to Samana Wasi where my parents were certain to be waiting for me. I was anxious to see them, so I hurried. Having crossed through some farms to save time, I arrived at the door of my house, by sunset of the fourth day. Before I could even knock, the door opened, and there stood my mother. She, as all mothers might, intuitively sensed the nearness of her son. I hugged and kissed her effusively. She was so excited that everyone else soon realized that I had arrived. My father came out of his room. We looked at each other and our eyes filled with tears. I hugged him in a way that I had never done before—just as the Brotherhood of the Sun did. There was no need for words.

Epilogue

The author witnessed the humble way in which the first edition in Spanish was published: a thousand copies, and on credit. Soon, a second and third edition were needed, and a fourth is presently on its way. To paraphrase the Epistles, nobody is prophet in his own land. So, by God's will, this book has been published in French, and now the English and German editions are also published in different places on this planet.

What is the secret of the rapid success of this book, which apparently is just one more among many esoteric and spiritual publications? It is its simple but strong message based on an experience at a geometric spot in the Peruvian Andes, where the Inti ("Sun" in the Quechua language) is recognized as the one that personifies the principal creator and legislator. However, this success is not only in a book that sells; but also, more importantly, "those who have ears to hear" have heard and there was an answer to the author's message in the following ways:

1. A link among the readers has emerged. Pilgrimage to the author's home in Cusco—the navel of the world—increases by the day. Also, letters are being sent to him from such remote places as El Nadir.

2. *Samana Wasi* ("The House of Rest" in Quechua) is now a dream come true only because of the premises donated by the author's family and the generosity of

readers from around the world. At the moment, the help given to these needy children is small, but the founder's faith can very well move mountains. As a true follower of his own teachings, the majority of the income that arrives from the book is devoted to the Samana Wasi Foundation.

Samana Wasi Foundation

Samana Wasi was founded in 1988, and it serves as a place of shelter for children living in the streets (*gamines*) and for lonely older people. It is located in the Holy Valley of the Incas, about 40 miles north-east of Cuzco. It was build on the family land of Antón Ponce de León Paiva. Antón himself founded the Foundation with his wife Regia. When his master Nina Soncco asked him to do so, he gave up his "normal" life–he had been a director of the television station in Cusco–and from then on worked only for Samana Wasi.

In an original approach, which departs from many of the ongoing projects in third world countries, Samana Wasi is intended to help the children and older people by means of a self-help program. In addition, Antón and his wife are not only concerned about giving shelter to those people; but also, they try to give them love and comfort. They believe this to be even more important than material support. The children that live with them will believe in themselves and in their own future.

The same holds true for older people. They who have the experience of a lifetime to offer will again become part of society. Here, they feel useful. The two forgotten parts of society–the elderly and the outcast children–cohabit in a new symbiotic environment. Everybody can learn from one other. "This family might fulfill the mystery that the one will grow wiser and the other grow younger." (Nina Soncco) Work, truthfulness, and honesty are the principles of Samana Wasi.

In accordance with the wisdom of the Incas received by Anton Ponce de León Paiva, the concept of Samana Wasi is based on three principles: Service, investigation, and personal development.

Service: The daily life is based on the principle that everybody helps the other. (Today I work for you; tomorrow for myself; all for one.) This is the basic precept for the adults looking after the children, for the family of Antón and Regia, as well as for the children and old people living in Samana Wasi. Everybody feels useful to the community. There is no room for racial, religious, or political discrimination. Everybody willing to help their brothers or sisters in need are welcome to do so.

Investigation: Samana Wasi is developing its own autonomous food system and medical treatment program. The participants in these programs are researching ancient and spiritual knowledge. Nina Soncco: " We have to rediscover the medical methods of our ancestors to use them for the benefit of our people. This includes the healing plants of our homeland and of other places. ... Similarly, the research in agriculture is needed, to find more and more natural foods." In addition to the rediscovery of ancient methods of agriculture and healing, this includes the consideration of the wisdom of the ancient Inca tradition, knowledge about life, and its inner meaning.

Personal development: The work for the community also serves the finding of one's self. Everybody—helper, helped, young and old—is requested to ask the question: "Who am I?" Through practical work, the inner harmony shall be regained.

Anton Pónce de León Paiva in Samana Wasi

"We intend to wake up the 'new human being' with awakened gifts and powers, who has found one's inner center, to be able to help the others." (Antón Ponce)

In the present first stage of Samana Wasi, twenty children find shelter. The next stage will increase this number, and will incorporate the aspect of investigation. The third stage will, according to the lessons given on the Fifth Day, integrate the thought of the Solar Brotherhood. Then Samana Wasi will also become a spiritual center.

"We are human beings of this world, we serve without borders those who need our help most." The Foundation Samana Wasi needs more support. For example, new house modules have to be built, in each of which ten children can live. The price for one module is $10,000. And, the children have to be fed and dressed.

If you want to help Samana Wasi, contact Antón Ponce directly.

Fundacion Samana Wasi
Antón Ponce de León Paiva
Casilla de Correo 575
Cusco, Peru

Footnotes

1 Four is a sacred number in the Andean cosmogony.
2 Pumacchupan is Quechua for the tail of the panther.
3 Pacchac is Quechua for abundantly flowing.
4 Sutoc is Quechua for scarcely flowing.
5 Korihuayrachina-the literal meaning in Quechua is the place where the gold is sifted by the wind. At the time of the conquest, the Spaniards began to dig here in search of the precious metal which they never found. To the Indians, "gold" was great wisdom.
6 On one occasion I had accompanied my father to the summit where there are very ancient rectangular constructions. Judging by the shape of the stone slabs, Karol Sieberg, a German investigator who has written about the Gran Pajaten and Amazon cultures, said that they are Telamons or something related to them.
7 "Kunkani" is Quechua for "neck."
8 A culi is a wrapping skirt.
9 Meaning head of light, mind of light, or head shining with wisdom
10 Chincanas is Quechua for labyrinths.
11 Chaska is Quechua for star; ñahui Quechua for eyes; Chaska ñahui, then, means star-like eyes, or eyes of light.
12 Nina Soncco is Quechua for heart of fire.
13 From a Latino Proverb.
14 Inti is Quechua for sun.
15 Creator of the World.

16   Cause of the Universe.

17   The Admirable Being.

18   An Incan drink made of fermented, germinated corn.

19   Apus are Andean protective deities; pronounced a-poo.

20   Pucu is a deep-baked, clay plate.

21   Noccan Kani is Quechua for I Am.

22   Hanan Pacha is Quechua for the place of beyond.

23   Ajay Pach is Quechua for the place of beyond, too.

24   Kay Pacha is Quechua for land of here.

25   Huaino is a Quechuan dance.

26   In Greek mythology, the food of the gods.

27   House of Rest.

28   Ama Ilulla, Ama Suwa, and Ama Kella.

29   Today for you, tomorrow for me.

30   All for one, in the realization of public works.

31   The exact mantra is a secret, and so has been obscured by the author.